"Social Media is a game-changer for the real estate brokerage industry. Get the Swanepoel Report and get on the right track today."

Kathy Howe
Educator, Arizona
Incoming President for the Real Estate Educators Association

"This is a must read!"

Alexander Chaparro
@properties

"Swanepoel is Real Estate's brightest leadership luminary."

Sherie Puffer
@sherriepuffer

"Thanks Stefan, you're a leader with education and your adaption to social media proves you are the king of real estate social media too."

John Reinhardt
President Fillmore Real Estate

"Thank you for all you do."

Jessica Fox
Realtor®, Wisconsin

"Stefan, your Reports are so useful. You always go way beyond the simple list of sites and portals."

Svetlana Stolyarova
Realtor® Cleveland

"Social Media will transform the real estate industry. Get started in the right direction by reading the Swanepoel Social Media Report."

Mike Bowler
Realtor® & Educator

SWANEPOEL SOCIAL MEDIA REPORT 2010

Authors
Stefan Swanepoel & Mel Aclaro

Research and Contributions by
Tinus Swanepoel & DJ Swanepoel

COPYRIGHT © 2009 by RealSure, Inc.

Printed in the United States of America with all rights reserved. Except as permitted under the United States Copyright Act of 1976, no part of this publication may be reproduced or distributed in any form or by any means, or stored in a database or retrieval system without the prior written permission of the publisher.

ISBN: 978-0-9704523-1-3

$ 79.00 USA
$ 89.00 CAN
€ 59.00 EUR

Other Publications by the Stefan Swanepoel:
Real Estate Handbook
A New Era in Real Estate
Swanepoel Top Real Estate Firms
Real Estate confronts Reality
Real Estate confronts Technology
Real Estate confronts the e-Consumer
Real Estate confronts the Banks
Real Estate confronts Profitability
Real Estate confronts Customer Acquisition
The Domino Effect
Real Estate confronts the Future
Real Estate confronts Bundled Services
Real Estate confronts Goal Setting vs. Business Planning
Real Estate confronts the Information Explosion
Swanepoel TRENDS Report 2006, 2007, 2008 & 2009

PUBLISHED BY
RealSure Publishing
PO Box 7259
Laguna Niguel
CA 92607

Publisher website:	RealSure.com
Report website:	RETrends.com
Bookstore website:	RealEstateBooks.org
Managing Editor:	Thomas M. Mitchell
Cover & Layout :	Laudi Centeno

Preface

Social Media is NOT a fad.

Social Media is a Game-changer.

Some say it may even be the biggest shift since the Industrial Revolution.

By 2010 Gen Y will outnumber Baby Boomers and 96% of them have already joined a social network. Have you?

Expect our lives to radically and exponentially be changed by Social Media and Networks over the next few years. Communication, collaboration, networking, marketing and sales—as we knew them last year—will NEVER be the same again.

The many traditional forms of media we have been using for decades are being eclipsed with a growth in membership numbers and adoption rates that we have never experienced before. Consumers no longer want or trust advertising to the same levels they did a decade ago. Today they want to talk to other consumers directly, creating a discussion and validating for themselves what they want or believe.

As always, the Swanepoel Reports serve to help guide you through the evaluation, discussion and implementation strategies of this new change.

Our very best to your continued success.

Stefan Swanepoel
On behalf of the Authors & Contributors
August 2009

Notice

Confidential Information

No confidential sources were used in this Report and no information identified as Confidential under any existing NDA was included without permission from the appropriate authorities. This Report is a result of research, articles that are readily available through the media, websites, Social Media networks, whitepapers, industry reports, notes taken during conventions and seminars and one-on-one discussions with a wide range of people.

Involvement

Although the author may serve as a consultant and advisor to companies mentioned in the Report, the author is not an officer or director of any of the companies referenced in this Report. For more information, visit realsure.com.

Accuracy, Sources and Surveys

As far as possible all statements, statistics and inferences were checked and although great care was undertaken to provide accurate and current information we cannot accept any responsibility for any liability, loss or risk that may be claimed or incurred as a consequence, directly or indirectly. All sources, publications and websites used to compile this Report are listed in the References section.

Examples and Disclaimer

References to any companies, products, services and websites do not constitute or imply endorsement and neither is any reference or absence of reference intend to harm, place at a disadvantage or in any other way affect any company or person. Information contained in this report should not be a substitute for common sense, thorough research and competent advice. Readers are urged to consult proper counsel or other authority regarding any points of law, finance, technology and business before proceeding and all conclusions expressed herein are subject to local, state and federal laws and regulations.

Copyright

Material in this report may be shared through a Creative Commons License and may be re-used as long as attribution is provided to this Report, and any original creator of any diagram or content used or referenced here within.

Acknowledgements

To the many, many, many awesome Social Media guru's and online friends that introduced us to the various services and nuances of Social Media. Thank you! (Our apologies if we missed anyone who feels they should have been included).

Brynn Allen	Joseph Ferrara	Mike Mueller
Chris Andersen	Jeff Fowler	Terri Murphy
Brad Andersohn	Maureen Francis	Nicole Nicolay
Rudy Bachraty	David Gibbons	Reggie Nicolay
Susie Blackmon	Brad Hanks	Derek Overbey
Kevin Boer	Robyn Hardy	Tawny Press
Mike Bowler	Matt Heaton	Randy Prothero
Chris Brogan	Liz Loadholt	Lani Rosales
Tom Braatz	Kathy Howe	Daniel Rothamel
Joel Burslem	Cheryl Johnson	Michael Russer
Sean Buvala	William Johnson	Kevin Sablan
Missy Caulk	Matt Jones	Ron & Alexandra Seigel
Paul Chaney	Pat Kitano	Sharon Simms
Todd Carpenter	Jon Lansner	Adam Singer
Alex Chaparro	Chris Lara	Brian Solis
Amy Chorew	Wendy Patton	Jacob Swodeck
Jeff Cornbett	Tom & Paula Pelton	Donald Teel
Jason Crouch	Michael McClure	Jesse Thomas
Kevin Cottrell	Mary McKnight	Frances Flynn Thorsen
Marc Davidson	Leili McKinley	Jeff Turner
Ken Deshaies	Kelly Mitchell	Rochelle, Haley & Chelsey Veturis
Joshua Dorkin	Jack Miller	Bill Wendell
Jeff Dowler	Jonathan Miller	Nicole Witt

A special thanks from Mel, to his wife and very patient best friend Tobi:
"I'd be more of a mess than the chaos I am today without you in my life."

A special thanks from Stefan to his awesome sons, Tinus & DJ:
"Thank you for not only introducing me to the world of Social Media but becoming such an integral part of this Report as well. I couldn't have done it without you!"

Table Of Contents

Chapter 1 - What is Social Media?

1.1 The Connectivity Revolution (Internet) 15

1.2 The Communication Revolution (Social Media) 16

1.3 Early Social Networks 17

1.4 Modern Social Media 17

1.5 The Power of One 19

1.6 The Long Tail 20

1.7 Summary of General Social Media Networks 21

1.8 Summary of Real Estate Social Media Networks 25

Chapter 2 - Where To Start

2.1 Determining the Landscape 31

2.2 Determining Motivation 31

2.3 Purpose Statement 31

2.4 How to Conduct Yourself 33

2.5 Cultural Awareness 35

2.6 Rules of Engagement 35

2.7 Managing Your Time 37

2.8 Measuring Your Success 38

2.9 Policies 38

Chapter 3 - Best Sites and Tools

3.1 Hubs-and-Spokes Framework 43

3.2 The Hub 43

3.3 The Outposts 43

3.4 Recommended Strategy 43

3.5 Your Blog 45

- Reveal Yourself
- Maximizing Your Blog

Table of Contents

3.6 Facebook 47

- The Culture
- Profiles and Pages
- Ways to Communicate
- * Maximizing Facebook

3.7 LinkedIn 51

- The Culture
- Online Resume
- Features
- Maximizing LinkedIn

3.8 Twitter 53

- The Culture
- Ways to Communicate
- Hashtags
- Maximizing Twitter

3.9 YouTube 56

- The Culture
- Channel Yourself
- Features
- Maximizing YouTube

Chapter 4 - Monitoring the Conversation

4.1 Components of Listening Posts 61

4.2 Manual Queries 62

4.3 RSS 63

4.4 Google Alerts 64

4.5 Message Board Alerts 65

4.6 Paid Monitoring Services 67

4.7 Social Media Optimization 67

Chapter 5 - Tying it all Together

    5.1 Dividing Up the Social Media Orchestra 71

    5.2 Communication Focus 73

    5.3 Multimedia Focus 74

    5.4 Collaboration Focus 75

    5.5 Other 76

    5.6 Finding the Social Balance 76

Chapter 6 - 10 Action Day Plan

    Day 1 80

    Day 2 81

    Day 3 82

    Day 4 83

    Day 5 84

    Day 6 85

    Day 7 86

    Day 8 87

    Day 9 88

    Day 10 89

References 93

Glossary of Social Media Terms 98

Glossary of Twitter Terms 102

About the Authors 105

Chapter 1

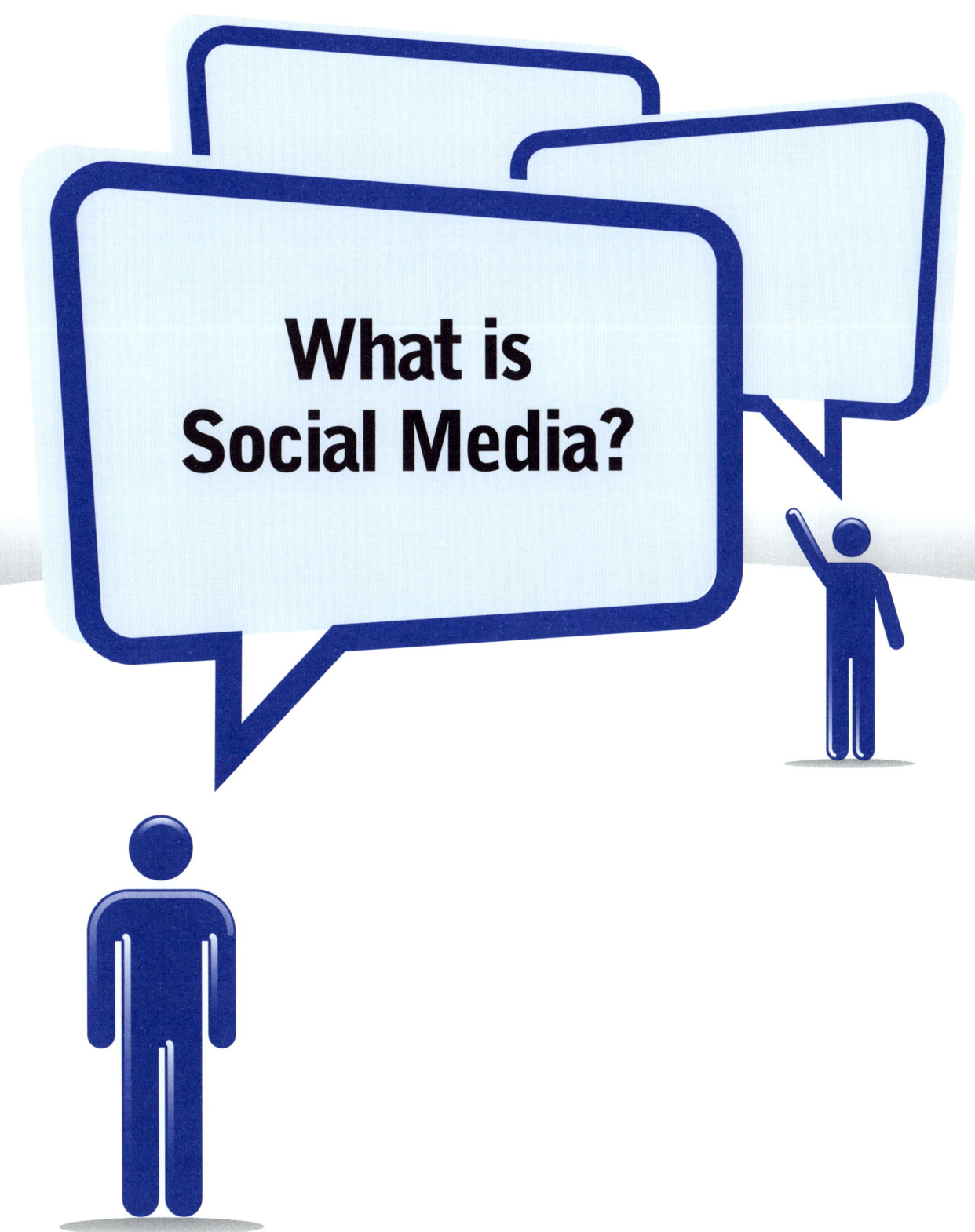

1.1 The Connectivity Revolution (Internet)

Social Media didn't just begin overnight. It's a natural and very important part of the evolution of the Internet.

The origins of the Internet can be traced back to 1957 with email arriving in 1971, the introduction of Usenet in 1979, Listserv in 1986, Internet Relay Chat or IRC in 1988 and personal websites including chat and discussion groups in 1991.

However, it was probably the introduction of the World Wide Web, Search Engines and the commercialization of the Internet in the early 1990s that led to the explosion of the Internet as we largely know it today. As the Internet continued to evolve during the 1990s the means of contacting individuals became easier. Instead of sending physical mail, electronic mail (email) began being used more widely. This method allowed individuals to send messages instantaneously around the globe at an insignificant fractional cost and it became the "silver bullet" that propelled the initial growth of the Internet; Web 1.0.

According to the International Data Corporation (idc.com) and Miniwatts Marketing Group (miniwatts.com), the number of Internet users has doubled every year since its public launch. By 1995 it had grown to include 23,000 websites of which 4,000 (17%) were real estate related.

After the dotcom crash of 2000 the public went through a period of disillusionment with the web; the consolidation of companies, products and services took place during the subsequent years. However, by 2004 the web had evolved into a new and more sophisticated communication tool; Web 2.0 was born. It changed the Internet from just providing the ability to gain information to a platform for interacting with anyone, anywhere, anytime via voice, video and messaging. Web 2.0 became a network for conversations with the activity of sharing forming the basis for many of those conversations. And that set the foundation for the launch of Social Media as it is known today.

In less than one-and-a-half decades the web evolved from browsing to searching to sharing.

- **Browsing**—To surf the web, users typed in the address of the destination they wanted to find like Realtor.com. Or they went to portals with links classified by a subject such as "real estate." As a result, companies spent big money on banner ads and branding campaigns to lure web surfers to their sites.

- **Searching**—As the web exploded it became harder for users to find what they wanted with any single website. Keywords ruled as web surfers clicked through lists of web results dished up by search engines. Google, with its simple look and super-smart algorithms, refined surfing and online advertising.

- **Sharing**—Today people are increasingly customizing personal websites, blogs and social network pages with little programs known as widgets. The real power of these simple services, created by individuals or large companies, is that they're shareable and can be distributed widely and easily.

> "Here's the problem: Social Media exists and Social Media is real. It gets used by people who are thinking about buying your product because it was created by the people who have already purchased your product."
>
> *-Dave Evans,*
> Social Media Marketing: An Hour A Day

Joe Kraus, Google's Director of Product Management stated that social networking is not new, there are just new ways of doing it. The common perception today is that networking is something we do at a specific site, but the realization is that being social is not a site—it's an activity. As it turns out, it's an activity that can be governed by principled and focused strategy. As a result it is important to prepare for a completely social web where buyers and sellers will expect to be part of the conversation. It's a concept that will grow in popularity in the real estate industry simply because the consumer increasingly wants it that way.

In simple terms, social networking companies have made it easy to stay in contact with friends and to make new connections through the sharing of content—the sociology of media. And for now, that's exactly what social networking and Social Media are all about.

1.2 The Communication Revolution (Social Media)

Communication has long been the cornerstone in the evolution of the Internet and with its growth, the method of making contact and communication with others has fundamentally changed. The "old paradigm" of sending a physical element of communication has changed from sending a letter or a fax, to sending an email or text, to posting a message to a blog in an online forum or social networking site.

The gestation of the process became evident in 1994 when Laurence Canter and Martha Siegel introduced the "Green Card" email, which is considered by many to be the first unsolicited email (spam) advertisement sent over the internet. Unknowingly they laid the foundation for using the Internet for potential business profit by simultaneously contacting large numbers of Internet users. Today's social networks have taken that concept to a whole new level.

These days the terms Social Media and social networks seem to be used interchangeably. But they are distinctly different and it's worth noting the basic difference before continuing. Wikipedia (wikipedia.com) provides the following definitions:

> • *A social network is a social structure made of … (generally, individuals or organizations) that is tied by one or more specific types of interdependency, such as friendship, kinship, financial exchange …or prestige.*
>
> • *Social media is online content created by people using highly accessible and scalable publishing technologies … (it represents) a shift in how people discover, read and share news, information and content … (it is) a fusion of sociology and technology…and (enables) the democratization of information, transforming people from content readers into publishers.*

Thus Social Media is a shift from the "one-to-many" broadcast model seen in newspapers, television, books and radio into a "many-to-many" model that is rooted in conversations between multiple individuals. Within the structure of social networks, Social Media lends itself to informational exchanges in which business reputations are defined by customer opinions and ratings, where press is delivered by independent bloggers and customers provide insights and direction for product development. It's a real time exchange of information in a collaborative format; Web 2.0.

WEB 2.0

Think about going out for an evening to attend a banquet or a party. The evening is still early and individuals are walking around making simple introductions. In the early 90s that's what the Internet was all about; it was making introductions to the world. As the 90s progressed, much like the evening banquet, discussions evolved and people began to ask questions; detailed questions. The simple questions—"who are you" and "what do you do"—have already been answered. Questions like "how can we work together" and "what do you think about …" started becoming key points of the conversation. This evolution also occurred within the Internet as its second stage emerged; the conversation. This was the transition between Web 1.0 and Web 2.0. Although the distinctive technology that signaled the arrival of Web 2.0 may be up for debate, there are some distinctions we can make between Web 1.0 and Web 2.0 (see table) and one of the most influential was the introduction of social networks.

Web 1.0	Web 2.0
Reading	Writing
Companies	Communities
Homepages	Blogs
Portals	RSS
Wired	Wireless
Owning	Sharing
Screen Scraping	APIs
Dialup	Broadband

1.3 Early Social Networks

Most studies cite the company SixDegrees (1997) as the first social network. At that time SixDegrees (deriving its name from the concept that no one in the world is more than six persons removed from anyone else) allowed users to create profiles, list their friends and even send messages or post bulletin board items to friends. A year later they allowed users to not only move freely through their lists of friends but also through the lists of their friends' friends, bringing the name of SixDegrees to fruition, but in 2001 it closed its doors due to lack of support.

By that time the concept of connecting like-minded people and providing them a place to congregate and communicate with one another had been established. It opened the door to using this new tool as a method of servicing individual group markets and niche groups serving specific communities such as the African American and Asian American communities in 1999 through the launch of the BlackPlanet (blackplanet.com) and AsianAvenue (asianavenue.com) social networks.

The most notable social networking site founded before the end of the twentieth century however was LiveJournal (livejournal.com). Founded in 1999 by Brad Fitzpatrick, LiveJournal was originally created as a method for him to keep his friends informed of his activities. It soon established itself as a virtual community-publishing platform allowing users to keep a blog, journal or diary. It was later restructured to become the social network for Russia.

By the turn of the century the concept of social networks was well established and the next six years would give birth to a new generation of Social Media sites. Friendster (friendster.com) launched in 2002, becoming the first large site to truly demonstrate the potential power of social networks when its membership grew to an astounding three million users within the first few months. But its "closed door" policy of permitting only a relatively short chain of friends to connect with was seen as a major limiting factor and further growth was stifled. The next generation of social networks would not make the same mistake.

1.4 Modern Social Media

In 2003 MySpace (myspace.com), Second Life (secondlife.com, Last.FM (last.fm), Delicious (delicious.com) and Hi5 (hi5.com) were launched. MySpace was originally intended to be an online data storage center, but by 2004 it had transitioned into a social networking site with robust media sharing features that had not previously been seen. There are few are membership restrictions (open to anyone over the age of 13) and users could add as many friends, personal profiles, blogs, photos, music and videos as they wanted; it was completely free. The correct mix allowed MySpace to become an instant hit among teenagers.

In July 2005 Rupert Murdoch's News Corporation (newscorp.com) acquired eUniverse (parent company of MySpace) for $580 million and of that total, $327 million—more than half—was attributed to the value of MySpace. Social Media was instantly validated as more than just a playground for teenagers. It was a viable marketing channel with tangible value. By June 2006 MySpace had become the most popular social networking site in the world; adding its 100 millionth user in August.

Chapter 1 | What is Social Media?

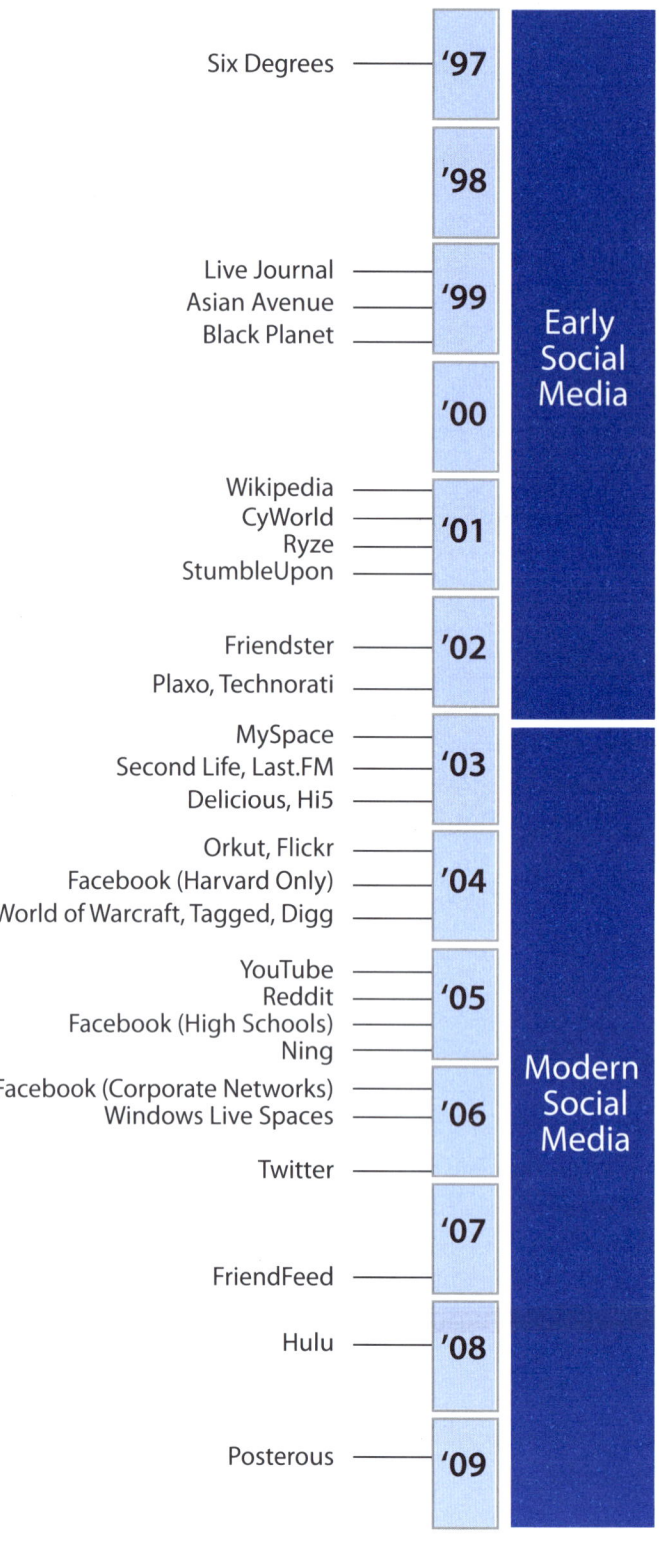

Almost overnight Social Media became the Internet's latest buzzword and the explosion was in full swing. From 2004 to 2006 most of the high profile social networking companies of today were launched: Flickr (flickr.com), Orkut (orkut.com), Digg (digg.com), Ning (ning.com), Reddit (reddit.com), YouTube (youtube.com) and of course, Facebook (facebook.com).

The creation of Facebook by Mark Zuckerberg was a milestone in Modern Social Media. Initially it was just intended to be a way for students at Harvard University to contact each other so that they could branch out and form friendships and study groups. Within 24 hours 1,200 Harvard students had signed up; one month later over half of the undergraduate population had a profile on Facebook. With such a strong following at Harvard, Facebook expanded its services to other college campuses all across America. By 2009 it joined MySpace as one of the few enormous Social Media networks; each boasting in excess of 250 million users.

> "Given that Social Networking Sites enable individuals to connect with one another, it is not surprising that they have become deeply embedded in user's lives."
>
> *-Danah Boyd*, University of California Berkeley
> *Nicole Ellison*, Michigan State University

Until recently the power to communicate with thousands was primarily bestowed to a limited group of media players: television broadcasters, radio stations and newspapers. They had the exclusive access to events and news and were the only effective distribution vehicle to users, readers and the public in general.

Now anyone with an Internet connection and a membership to a large Social Media site has the capability of reaching thousands of people inexpensively and quickly. This is changing the whole

DID YOU KNOW!

If Facebook and MySpace were their own countries they would be ranked the 4th and 5th most populous countries in the world, just behind the U.S. with each holding approximately three percent of the world's population.

1.5 The Power of One

Increasingly, consumers want to talk to consumers. According to Socialnomics (socialnomics.net), only 14% of consumers trust advertisements, whereas 78% trust peer recommendations. Consumers no longer trust advertising and marketers as they used to. Social Media has now created a simple connection whereby millions of consumers can talk with each other and share information about individuals, companies and their services—you and your company.

media structure of how we discover, obtain and share information. According to comScore (comScore.com), vkontakte.ru—a social network in Russia—has the most engaged audience in the world with visitors spending 6.6 hours viewing 1,307 pages per person per month. Suddenly the individual consumer has gained the potential power of a TV or radio broadcaster, albeit this ability does not equate to quality or acceptance. Anyone can talk to anyone and share his or her experiences, but the power or influence is not given or attained freely.

Respect, reputation and reach still have to be earned, as was the case for media professionals. In the world of Social Media, creating a credible "brand" requires building a relationship of trust with followers/friends/readers as a person with integrity that provides value-added quality content.

Real estate professionals have an excellent opportunity to take advantage of this phenomenon by creating meaningful content and releasing it to their consumers and potential clients through blogs, online communities, wikis and social networks. How big is this opportunity? Forrester Research (forrester.com) reported in 2007 that only 18% of all online Americans actually create content or publish an article or a blog at least once a month; the opportunity is huge but success doesn't come easily.

Used correctly, online communities can become powerful tools in the hands of a real estate professional. They are venues for providing content that will benefit the home buying or home selling consumer. Social networks become groups of individuals that have trust in one another because of outside relationships or by having developed trust in each other over time through shared experiences (and shared information). As a result, taking the lead in providing useful, quality content that is relevant to the specific network through "threads" and "online discussions" is the key to assuming a leadership role within a network.

The bottom line—it's the smart brokers and agents that will be the ones that develop a strategy to maximize this new power (more on "how" in later chapters).

DID YOU KNOW!

Facebook is the third most visited website in the world according to Hitwise. It follows Google and Yahoo! Mail, which are first and second respectively.

The key to establishing a position of influence online lies in the ability to successfully assess the social activities and needs of your market. Previously the sharing of information was primarily through email and website advertising; now it's through participation on Social Media sites. It's all about freely providing quality content and then inviting followers/friends/clients within the social network to choose their involvement rather than forcing them to participate. The consumer response then becomes one of subsequent interest that is "pulled" by the prospective consumer rather than reacting to content that is "pushed" to them.

1.6 The Long Tail

The Long Tail is a concept used to describe the strategy of some businesses such as Amazon (amazon.com) to sell a large number of unique items in small quantities. However, online retail takes on a new meaning with Social Media. In online Social Media the "Long Tail of Popularity" refers to the influences of individuals relative to one another. According to a Harvard study of 300,000 Twitter users, 10% of the users generated more than 90% of the content. This means that for Twitter, with over 18 million users, 1.8 million users posted over six million tweets (microblog posts).

However staggering those numbers may appear, the key point is that it costs literally nothing to create content, and once that content is created it is instantly available for others to enjoy. That low cost means that it doesn't matter if it's not read by millions of people. According to HubSpot (hubspot.com), even on Twitter just 35% of the users have 10 or fewer friends. According to another study, the top 10 keywords (used when searching) represent 19.5% of search traffic, whereas the Long Tail represents 80.5%.

The Long Tail of Popularity therefore suggests that anyone can find a home in Social Media and that you don't need to be a superstar to be able to communicate, collaborate and influence others.

1.7 Summary of General Social Media Networks

In Section 3 there is a discussion of the Top 5 Social Media sites that real estate professionals should focus on with suggestions on how to become involved with each and maximize the benefits of these new platforms. But first, here is a short summary of the most popular Social Media, networks, communities and blogs:

- **Delicious** (delicious.com)—A social bookmarking website that allows users to post URLs to various other websites. Through a variety of features such as saving bookmarks, automated bookmark organization and bookmark sharing, Delicious operates as a simple collection that is accessible anywhere, anytime. It also gives the user access to a collective search feature that searches all the bookmarks contained within Delicious and displays the most bookmarked results, based on the number of people that have bookmarked a particular site. This indicates not only the websites that are relevant but also those that are highly valued among similar users.

- **Digg** (digg.com)—A social news website where users add headlines and links to articles they find interesting. The principal feature of Digg is a voting system surrounding the submitted articles, links or stories. Its readers review entries and, based on preference, they either "digg" or "bury" an article, referring to whether the entry is "liked" or "disliked." The more votes a story gets, the more prominently it is displayed on the site.

- **Facebook** (facebook.com)—A social networking site that enables users to connect with friends and family. Through a variety of features, such as wall posting, photo tagging, group creation and participation and events notification, Facebook excels at connecting users with friends and keeping them in touch by providing a platform through which they can easily create and/or share online media and leave notes about it with each other. It draws people in to spend hour after hour on the site by not only giving them access to their friends' information but allowing them to leave notes on "the Wall," send messages, share photos, upload or link to videos, see who they have befriended, etc.

- **Flickr** (flickr.com)—A picture and video-sharing site that allows users to post pictures, upload short video clips, edit photos and, to a limited extent, write blogs. Flickr organizes images using tags that allow users to create collections and sets of pictures or videos. Additional features allow them to share where their photos and videos were taken as well as create products such as photo books, framed prints and DVD's from uploaded photos. It has been widely adopted as a primary storage location for photos, especially in the blogging community.

- **Friendfeed** (friendfeed.com)—A real-time aggregator that consolidates comments and posts from Social Media, networking and bookmarking sites and RSS (Really Simple Syndication) feeds into one easy to manage and view service. Friendfeed was acquired by Facebook in 2009.

Chapter 1 | What is Social Media?

SOCIAL MEDIA NETWORKS

Source: RealSure

- **Last.fm** (last.fm)—An Internet radio and music community site that allows users to create a profile, user groups and events surrounding music. By listening to music through Last. fm a user is able to create a musical profile based upon personal preferences and habits. This in turn generates suggested music, people, journal entries and events that are tailored to the individual user.

- **LinkedIn** (linkedin.com)—A social networking site designed as a place for business professionals to build an online network of contacts. This professional network focuses on the "gated-access" approach where trust among its users is determined by allowing connections among individuals to be established based on either a pre-existing relationship or contact introductions. Additional features such as job search or job postings can also be found.

- **MySpace** (myspace.com)—A social networking site that has, over time, become an online club for teenagers and the entertainment industry. Operating as one of the most versatile and open social networks, MySpace allows for complete profile customization, including backgrounds, layouts, music, etc. It is also home to upcoming artists and musicians that want to connect to fans. However, due to the exceptionally large teen membership it has evolved as a teen playground, characterized as a mishmash of modern (social) media; rich with music, video and comedy.

- **Ning** (ning.com)—A social network platform that enables users to build their own custom social networks. By allowing users to create networks that cater to any need, topic, expertise or membership base, Ning has assumed the title of the mother of modern niche networks. Additional customization allows for ad control, additional storage and non-Ning URL hosting.

- **Orkut** (orkut.com)—A social networking service designed for individuals to meet new people and maintain current relationships. Its most popular user base is Brazilian as a result of a viral campaign that generated popularity in that country. Orkut is similar to many other social networks and is focused around communities, themes and scrapbooking. It also integrated into Google, enabling a chat feature as well as file sharing through the network.

- **Reddit** (reddit.com)—A social news site that allows users to post links to content on the Internet. Links are then voted upon, resulting in an increase in their prominence on the Reddit home page. Additional features include forums that allow users to examine and discuss the posted links and vote for or against comments relating to any particular link.

- **Second Life** (secondlife.com)—A virtual world that allows members to create an online persona known as an "avatar." Through their avatar users can explore the world, interact in society, shop, visit entertainment events and do essentially everything they might in the real world—including buy and sell real estate. Many companies have a presence in Second Life including Intel, Coca-Cola, Coldwell Banker and Bank of America.

- **Squidoo** (squidoo.com)—A network site built and maintained by people who have expertise in a certain area and want to share that knowledge with others. On the Squidoo network each expert's site is called a "lens." Lenses operate much like blog posts; however a key distinction is that they focus on a single subject. Additional features allow users to create multimedia pages without the necessity of learning html or web design.

- **StumbleUpon** (stumbleupon.com)–An Internet community that uses peer and social networking principles to filter content when searching for information. Whenever a user clicks "Stumble," a new webpage is displayed based on the preferences. As such, StumbleUpon is considered a recommendation engine where ratings from users form collaborative opinions on website quality and relevant content.

- **Tagged** (tagged.com)—A social networking site that allows users to build and customize profiles, send messages, write comments, post bulletins, browse photos, watch videos and play games.

- **Technorati** (technorati.com)—An engine for searching blogs. It indexes millions of blog posts in real time and tracks not only the authority and influence of blogs, but it's also the most comprehensive and current index of who and what is most popular in the blogosphere. Technorati's rating system categorizes results based on tags that authors place on their websites.

> **"We now have indisputable proof that online marketing, YouTube and Twitter and all that they encompass, is meaningful and has arrived. We are seeing real consequences to a mistake. If [social networks] didn't matter, you wouldn't see this type of reaction from consumers."**
>
> Danah Boyd, University of California Berkeley
> Nicole Ellision - Michigan State University

Chapter 1 | What is Social Media?

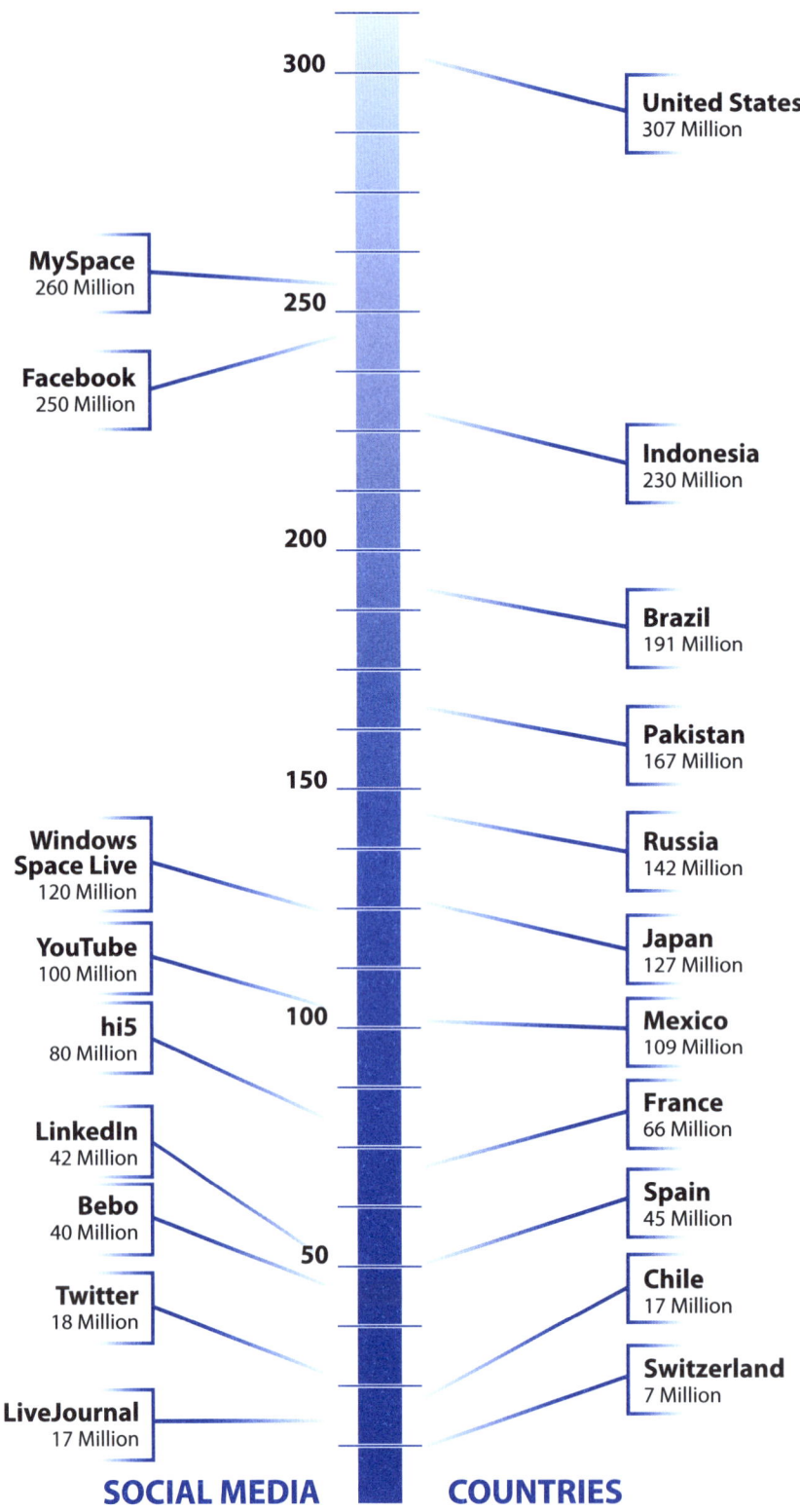

Source: RealSure

- **Twitter** (twitter.com)—A Microblogging (short blogging entries/posts) community site with posts limited to 140 characters. These short posts, or "tweets," as they have come to be known, are quickly sent to a user's entire following or collection of friends. Although Twitter is merely a rising star in the Social Media space, the simplicity of the site along with its messaging capabilities has allowed it to move into the realm of news broadcasting since user tweets often break the news before it airs in the mainstream media.

- **Windows Live Spaces** (spaces.live.com)—A blogging and social networking platform that includes blogs, photos, lists, friends, profiles and comment sections known as guestbooks. WLSpaces focuses primarily on reaching out to others through the blogging system encouraging users to publish their thoughts. It is widely considered to be the modern social diary.

- **YouTube** (youtube.com)—A video-sharing network. It allows its members to publish and communicate via videos; generally limited to 10 minutes. Due to the large amount of users, variety of videos and the ability to "embed" (share) videos that have been uploaded to YouTube into other websites, YouTube has become a popular destination when searching for anything video related and is now the #2 search engine in the world. Think of YouTube as the Facebook or MySpace of the video world.

1.8 Summary of Real Estate Social Media Networks

- **ActiveRain** (activerain.com)—A blogging and social networking platform that includes blogs, profiles channels and comment sections. ActiveRain focuses primarily on reaching out to others through blogging, encouraging users to publish their thoughts and comments or refer others to their site and obtain higher rankings through an interaction-point-based system. It is widely considered to be the largest Social Media site in the real estate industry.

- **BiggerPockets** (biggerpockets.com)—A blogging and forum-based social network platform with a focus on the business of real estate and real estate investing. BiggerPockets seeks to educate members through its articles, blogs and forums without interruption from unwanted solicitation and by providing resources to enhance real estate knowledge.

> "A band with no history can get 40,000 people looking at its video just by getting on the site [MySpace] and doing some work. It's a strong incentive. The technology has changed so much in the past six or seven years. You can make a video cheaply. The quality may be lacking, but I think fans get excited when they discover a band that's made its own record or video. They're the first to see them underground."
>
> *-Tom Anderson*
> Cofounder, MySpace

- **Broker Agent Social** (brokeragentsocial.com)—A new social networking community for agents, brokers, marketing specialists and other professionals that want to provide support. BrokerAgentSocial includes features such as blogging, video-sharing, event coordination, polling and forums.

- **Inman Community** (inman.com)—A division of Inman News, a real estate news service that focuses on blogging, group based discussions and collaborations through their wiki. Other features on Inman Community include a marketplace and a job search function based on location.

TOP 30 GLOBAL SOCIAL MEDIA NETWORKS

Category/Users/Viewers	Name	Type/Focus	Type/Focus
Enormous Networks (250 Million+)	Facebook	General	Global
	MySpace	Mainly Teens	Global
	YouTube	Video	Global
	QQ	General	China
Very Large Networks (50-150 Million)	Windows Live Spaces	Blogging	Global
	Friendster	General	Mainly Asia
	hi5	General	Mainly Asia, Africa, Latin America
	Tagged	General	United States
	Orkut	General	India and Brazil
	Habbo	Mainly Teens	Global
	Flixster	Movies	Northern America
	Mylife	Connections	Northern America & Europe
	Classmates	School/Work/Military	Global
Large Mainly Regional Networks (20-50 Million)	LinkedIn	Business	Mainly Europe and Canda
	51	General	China
	Baidu	General	China
	Netlog	General	Northern America, Europe & Australia
	Bebo	General	Mainly Russia
	V Kontakte	General	Mainly Russia
	Odnoklassniki	General	Mainly Europe
	Badoo	General	Global
	AdultFriendFinder	Dating	Global
	Last.fm	Music	Global
	MyHeritage	Genealogy	Global
	Xanga	Blogging	Global
	Twitter	Music, Video, Photos	Global
	imeem	Microblogging	United States
	Xiaonei	General	China
	Skyrock	General	Mainly Europe & Canada
	Mixi	General	Japan

Source: RealSure

- **Real Estate Wiki** (realestatewiki.com)—An online wiki and collaboration platform that focuses on all real estate related information. Real Estate Wiki offers information in a variety of categories including a glossary, real estate professionals, local community information and international real estate information. It also offers the use of a Wiki Widget that enables the search of the wiki from any website.

- **RealSeekR** (realseekr.com)—A blended networking platform combining real estate listings, photos and video, blogging, networking and live chat. RealSeekR's Live Chat enables consumers to speak immediately with the listing agent or other professionals about a particular house or housing in general. Other multimedia features can be utilized to enhance listings with video tours and video podcasts.

- **RealTown** (realtown.com)—A blogging and networking platform with features that include groups, communities, blogs, articles and an online store. Other features such as Ask the Expert give registered users the ability to pose questions that are most frequently answered by an expert in the RealTown network.

- **Trulia Voices** (trulia.com/voices)—A division of Trulia and operates as a community blogging platform where individuals can find advice and opinions and share knowledge with local experts. Trulia Voices also allows you to post questions and answers to topics, blog and subscribe to alerts.

2.1 Determining the Landscape

A couple of years ago Karl Fisch, a technology director in Colorado, and Scott McLeod, a professor at Iowa State University, produced a video titled *Did You Know; Shift Happens*. One of the key messages communicated so poignantly is the notion that: *We are living in exponential times.* Panels in their video extolling banners like, *we are currently preparing students for jobs that don't yet exist …using technologies that haven't been invented* and *…in order to solve problems we don't even know are problems yet,* give us a feeling for the pace of change and our limited resources for keeping up.

In the *Conversation Prism*, creators Brian Solis and Jesse Thomas spice the panorama by succinctly illustrating a spectrum of platforms associated with numerous types of online conversations, blogs, micromedia, lifestreams, social networks, video, events, music, photos and much more.

This is a huge landscape and it begs the question: *Where do I begin?*

2.2 Determining Motivation

Where to begin with Social Media doesn't start with a recommendation of Social Media platforms, it begins with determining your motivation.

Borrowing from Stephen Covey's philosophies about *being proactive and beginning with the end in mind*, it is important that you have a clear and concise motivation and vision of why you are getting involved with Social Media. Otherwise you run the risk of falling into the trap of *aimless exploration*.

Social Media has endless benefits in expanding your circle of influence, promoting your brand, gaining new customers and even conducting actual transactions. However, it comes at a price—time. *Your time.*

Social networking is not a task that you should initially automate or delegate because at the very core of Social Media is personal connectivity and relationship building. Thus, before you start, make sure you are ready and motivated.

> **"**As a component of Social Media, trust seems likely to follow in the word-of-mouth-based exchanges that occur in the context of Social Media.**"**
>
> *–Dave Evans,*
> Social Media Marketing: An Hour A Day

2.3 Purpose Statement

The Steps

Your Social Media strategy should begin with a statement of purpose. Armed with that you'll be in a better position to evaluate which platforms are the right ones in which to invest your time. And, more to the point, which communities and/or groups within each community should you commit your time and resources.

The steps should include:

Step 1: What is it that you do?

Unless you already know the niche that you fill and why people come to you, try approaching these steps as a brainstorming activity. Take no more than five minutes to quickly list all the things you do in your real estate business.

Chapter 2 | Where to Start?

THE CONVERSATION PRISM

Created by Brian Solis & Jesse Thomas
Source: theconversationprism.com

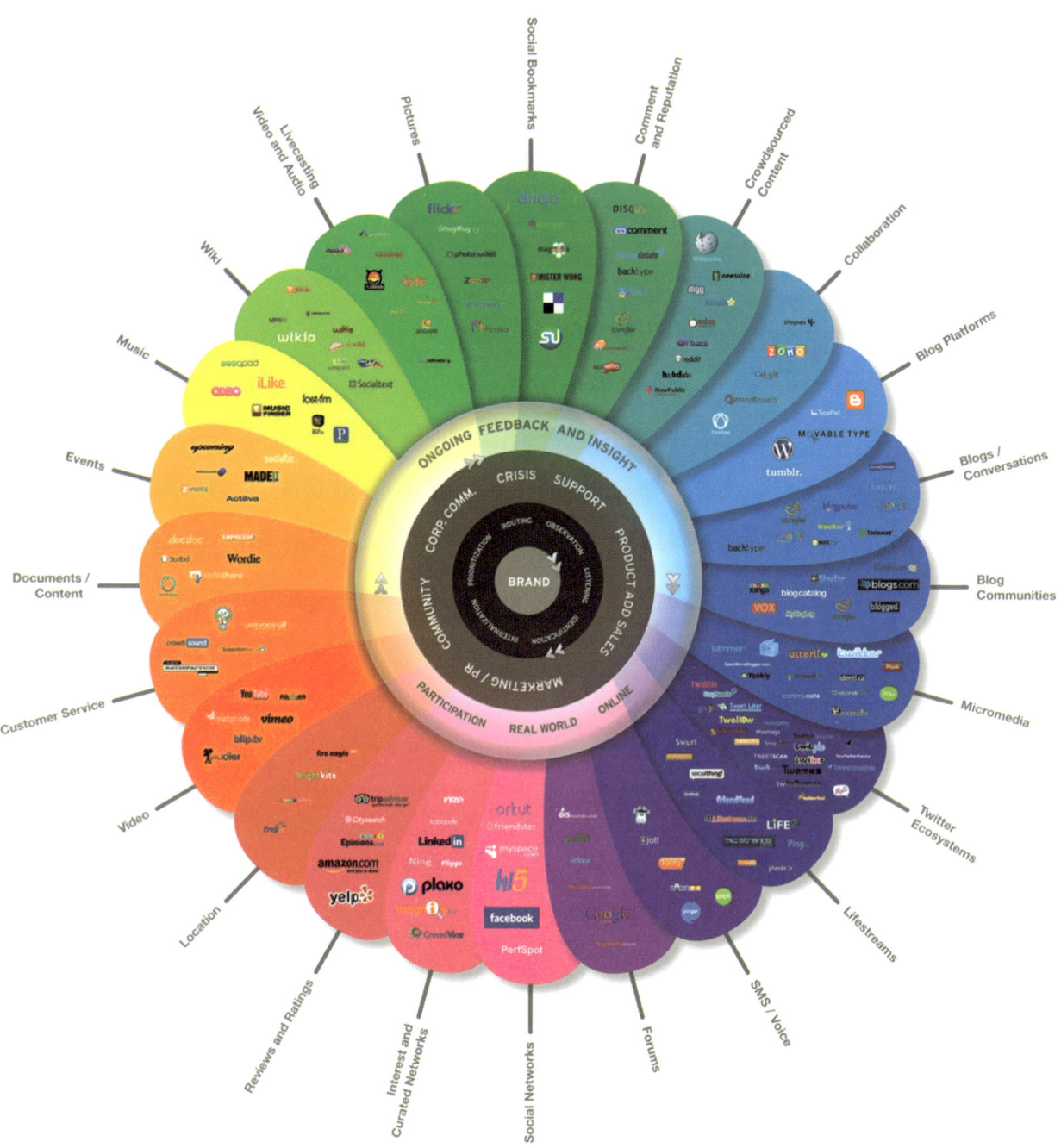

Step 2: For whom do you do what you do?

Take another look at your list and pick the nouns representing people or groups, and don't be shy about adding to your list if something new comes to mind.

Step 3: How do you do what you do?

Continue the process of refining the list from Step 2, only this time focus on descriptive words that you would use to describe your unique approach to servicing your customers.

Step 4: Assemble the pieces

As a final exercise, try forming a few sentences using some of the nouns, verbs and adjectives developed in the previous steps. This part of the exercise will be trial-and-error and you will likely follow an iterative process as you combine words into meaningful statements that ultimately resonate with what you feel is true about the value you and your business add to the community.

With your purpose clearly defined, use this process later when you find yourself wading into the online social stream and begin experiencing the fuzzy logic of shortcuts, impersonal automation and time allocation. These are distractions of the type that are sometimes vilified in the social web as they tempt you to consider automation in building lots of followers quickly, automating your "DMs" (Direct Message), or to blindly request a connection with another professional with nothing more to go on than a solicitation as seen on LinkedIn that states …you are a person I trust.

The purpose of your involvement with social networks and Social Media will significantly dictate how you get involved, the networks in which you elect to participate and what kind of information or media you should post.

2.4 How to Conduct Yourself

Your Profile

Your presence will typically be shown in the form of a network profile (your public face), created in the description of your participation. Think of this latter point as proof of your character through your actions online. You need commitment to both.

In other words, don't just sign up for a network account on LinkedIn or Facebook with the intent of engaging in conversations without taking the time to polish a complete profile in that network. At the end of the day, people still prefer to engage in conversations with others whom they can see and put a face to. It won't serve you well to have a prospect finally click-through with interest in you or your brand, only to be confronted with a default picture and minimal profile.

Positioning Yourself (Finding Your Spot)

When participating in Social Media you will have various opportunities to create a persona. Before doing so you should clearly decide how you want the world to view you. To achieve this, ask yourself the following questions:

- Are you someone who is using Social Media for personal or professional use?
- If you're using Social Media for professional use, what information are you presenting?
- Are you an individual that offers quotes or frivolous information or do you provide real and relevant content?
- Do you respond to people or ignore people?
- Who are you connecting with?
- What do you want your online experience to be like?
- How do others view you?

It's important that you know what your motivation is for joining (business, social, networking, etc.) and whether you will want to create a professional or a personal profile.

Take Away
- Profile yourself
- Find synergies
- Find your market

Building a Brand (Adding Value to Your Spot)

After you have decided what your positioning is, the next step is to decide what brand you will be building online. Consistency is important and attaching the desired identifying image helps in placing and posturing yourself. For example, you can be an expert in anything—a topic, an area, etc.—or you don't have to be an expert at all, just everyone's friend. Regardless of what you choose for your goal, building your brand will require you to standardize and unite the message behind your brand; photo, logo, content, website, etc. In the end, all these elements must portray a unified message.

Take Away
- Offer help
- Be consistent
- Add value

Conveying Authenticity (Ensuring Your Spot is Sincere)

As social networks are personal venues for connecting one person directly with another, it is important to create online relationships that are built on mutual respect and trust. Because users may never physically meet, and therefore not have the opportunity to build the confidence that you are who you say you are, you need to demonstrate online that you are someone worth taking the time to build a relationship with. To be authentic in Social Media requires users to be sincere and engaging.

Take Away
- Be real
- Be sincere
- Be engaging

Create a Following (Making Your Spot Popular)

To create a following in Social Media you have to "give" more than you "take." Connect with like-minded people that you can initially relate to and with whom you share common interests. If you interact with your followers and friends by actively creating discussions and continually engaging with others in the community, others will, in turn, be compelled to follow you.

Take Away
- Give more than you take
- Stay relevant
- Acknowledge others

Creating a Sales Pipeline (Making Your Spot Count)

Sales follow trust, confidence and value. Similar to shopping in a mall, some interaction or a recommendation creates trust. Thereafter customers need to first be aware of a store. Then, after gaining more information, they may enter and browse through the product selection. Often they might ask for help or more information and you should be ready and willing to provide it. Use Social Media to guide your potential customers to your offerings. Don't try and sell them. Let them "pull" the information they need.

As many Social Media sites only allow short or limited messaging such as Twitter (140 characters) you will need to direct potential customers to your blog or website where you have more space and control in order to more comprehensively describe your products and services.

Take Away
- Don't sell – Inform
- Don't sell – Redirect
- Don't sell – Guide them

Synopsis

It's been said that new economics have emerged that are built around social currency. To build up an account you need only to demonstrate commitment to a practice of helping others online, reposting or retweeting (RT) beneficial messages from your contacts and occasionally helping to make someone else an online hero by talking them up.

Paradoxically, the more selfless your actions the more attention you will draw to yourself. In that regard, the community will demand a way of learning more about who you are. Hence it's important to pay attention to having a complete profile that invites new Outpost friends to a Hub that explains more about your values, interests and passions. This applies to each of the social network outposts in which you stake a foothold.

2.5 Cultural Awareness

Another thing to consider is the fact that each social network has its own *culture*.

Culture translates to "cultivate;" a term having various meanings. For example it can be interpreted as cultivating taste, as in fine arts, or in the way intended here, *a set of shared attitudes, values and practices that characterize an organization or group.*

What this implies is that you have to dress and speak for the occasion. You wouldn't want to show up to a business meeting dressed for a barbecue. Nor would you risk alienating new business contacts by sharing with them old high school pictures, vacation photos or videos from occasions that you would rather forget. Keep this in mind when you join any network.

2.6 Rules of Engagement

Just as it's important to know the rules of the road and driving etiquette before venturing on the open highways, so it is equally important that you have an understanding of the customs of Social Media. Although no hard legal rules exist, there are many good manners to follow if you want the vast crowds of the Social Media world to follow you.

- **Give More Than You Take.** The more you contribute to conversations and discussions, the more people will recognize your name and what you stand for. Over time you will establish credibility and build value. Remember the well-known adage, *the more you care, the more you share.*

- **Respect.** Be respectful of the community, the members, the group's overall goals, etc. Social Media is a participatory sport and that means that you are one of many. People can chose to communicate with you or they can chose to ignore you. Treat others as you want to be treated.

- **Listen.** Listening and receiving comments and feedback are two of the greatest strengths of Social Media. They represent first-hand interaction with your customer. By listening to them you gain unfiltered feedback about your products and market.

- **Respond.** When people comment or leave messages for you it's only polite to respond in a timely fashion. By responding you are validating to the online community that you are an individual who values and acknowledges others. This adds to your credibility as an individual.

- **Build Relationships.** It's called social networking for a reason. Make sure you build relationships with everyone that communicates with you; establish conversations, ask questions, respond to questions, etc. Discussions and relationships encourage people to return to your page, thereby building a meaningful community.

- **Be Authentic and Transparent.** Be sincere and honest; be yourself. With Social Media displaying your profile, message and comments it is critical to your success that you are genuine and dependable.

- **Do Not Become a Nuisance.** It's generally agreed that spamming is bad, but it's also important to avoid becoming a Keyboard Gangster, Envelope Pusher or a Social Saboteur.

    i. <u>Keyboard Gangsters</u> are individuals that commonly act tough and disrespectful. They are really just spammers and are constantly found spamming message boards or discussions with derogatory comments and insults.

    ii. <u>Envelope Pushers</u> are individuals that constantly ask for help. They are also referred to as the beggars of the Social Media world that tend to flood your inbox with requests.

    iii. <u>Social Saboteurs</u> are individuals that often don't pay attention to discussions and often respond with irrelevant information manipulating the discussion in a different direction. They often seek to ruin or slow down the discussion by posting negative comments such as: I hate ---, don't buy it.

- **Collaborate.** Social Media is a collective medium. This means that it uses the knowledge or wisdom of the whole group; not just a single individual. For that reason, information obtained in Social Media on Wikis or reviews is seldom entirely wrong. On the other hand, it's often not 100% right. As a result, there is a strong need to work together, updating and constantly adding value to improve the quality of the content.

- **Consider Opportunities in the Long Tail.** In Social Media, every service offering has some degree of value. It's not always wise to just focus on the few services that command a high frequency of interest among a few niche groups and the requisite competition that introduces other service providers. As technology continues to erode communication barriers, value will also come from the many niche groups in "the tail" that demonstrate interest in services that conventional (competing) service providers would otherwise consider having little value.

- **Add Value.** Every member of a community must contribute his or her fair share. What is your contribution? Remember that contributions come in many different shapes and actions: providing information, being a resource, answering questions and redistributing information.

DID YOU KNOW!

Most Internet providers only allow you to send a few hundred emails in a day. By using Social Media sites such as Facebook you can reach thousands of individuals instantly. Better yet, you won't get any bounce back emails.

2.7 Managing Your Time

Being effective with Social Media can be difficult, as you will initially be struggling with questions such as:

- How many hours should I spend on Social Media per day?
- What activities will bring me the most value?
- Which Social Media Platforms should I pick—I can't do them all?

To maximize your participation in Business and Social Networks you need to use your time effectively.

Start by spending 30 – 45 minutes each day on Social Media in intervals of 15 minutes spread throughout the day. This will give you time to establish discussions and respond to previous posts. It will also give you time to add more friends and catch up on a few messages.

Establish the goals that are important for you before you dive into Social Media. Are you looking to build a small circle of quality friends online, build or expand an existing brand online, drive eye-balls and traffic to your website, do actual sales or have the most followers irrespective of who they may be? Although these goals may all sound similar, there is a significant difference in how and where you should spend time achieving each of them. Toward the end of this Report there is more detail on how you can achieve many of these different goals and what different tools or applications are available.

Social Media is all about engaging others in helpful conversation, so it should come as no surprise that to be effective you will need to communicate on a regular basis. However, try to cap the amount of time spent to approximately an hour a day and avoid using mobile applications for Facebook or Twitter during the course of the day to tell everyone what may be happening at any point in time. Keep the majority of your tweets and postings business related and professional. Allocate time throughout the day: 15 minutes early in the morning, 15 minutes half way through the day and 30 minutes in the evening.

> **"The key is to be true to your community's norms and values. You can't just force yourself on people and try to sell them something they don't want. You have to find ways to add value to your members' lives while being consistent with your brand's identity."**
>
> *–Chris DeWolfe*
> Cofounder, MySpace

Staying Focused

To maximize your participation in Business and Social Networks you need to focus your efforts on the right activities.

Social Media can very quickly gobble up a lot more time than you ever thought you were going to spend on it. To avoid that trap, decide what activities will achieve your desired results. Here are a few examples of how to allocate your time:

- **Adding new friends/ followers**—Do this manually, carefully selecting your friends and followers will build a quality following. It will take a longer time than by using an assistant or an application to automatically add friends/followers. They will allow you to grow your base much faster but you may find that you have many "questionable" friends and followers, and you will have to clean up your database on a regular basis.

- **Posting tweets or articles**—Again, if you do this personally you will only be able to do a few a day, but you will be able to add meaningful, relevant and quality content. If, on the other hand, you delegate this task to an assistant, or post standard messages on pre-determined intervals, use auto responders or constantly re-tweet every message, the value of your site or page will decline. Remember, Social Media is all about building online relationships and your contacts want to build that relationship with you, not with a computer.

- **Adding value to another person's tweet or post**—If you want to build a strong following and thus be effective online you need to, from day one, establish a human connection. You have to communicate with your circle of friends and/or followers. Read the tweets or posts of others and comment on them, visit their wall and leave a message and re-tweet good messages and share them with your friends. Become a real segment of the community by giving more than you take.

> **"The good news about social media is the enormous potential to create new conversations online, build brand awareness, and attract new business."**

-Frances Flynn Thorsen
Real Estate Social Media Policies

2.8 Measuring Your Success

If your purpose is to use Social Media for business, then you no doubt would like to measure the success you enjoy from it and be able to determine your return on investment (ROI).

First, let's start by stating that Social Media is less akin to advertising than it is to building interest through relationships. Positioning, relationship building and consultative sales have more of a positive impact than the "in your face" approach. With that said, measuring ROI in economic and financial terms could, in many cases, be very difficult. Ideally we would like to measure success in terms that gauge to what extent our efforts have impacted the bottom line. Such metrics should include financial measures like:

- Profitability
- Increased sales
- Reductions in cost
- Agent productivity by sales volume
- Optimal list-to-sales price ratios
- Reductions in number of expired listings per branch

Over time the service providers of analytics will get better at compiling the social media indicators that map to "hard" (financial) metrics at the brokerage level. Such a degree of analysis, when compared to initial outlays, will do wonders for developing sophisticated presentations of "ROI dashboards." Until that time, such financial dashboards won't likely be achievable without significant manual effort by managers—often with the help of external social media business consultants—to define quantifiable business objectives, behavior changes and key performance indicators that map to specific dollars.

There are, however, still a number of ways to gauge— at least in non-financial terms— whether or not you are using the Social Media platform effectively. The traditional approach to measurement involves tracking numerical values such as number of friends, followers, views, etc. Online analytics services such as those provided through Google Analytics (google.com/analytics), Google Adwords (adwords.google.com), Yahoo Web Analytics (web.analytics.yahoo.com), Radian6 (radian6.com), HubSpot (hubspot.com) and others have made it very easy to gather basic information. Sophisticated compilation engines have automated the creation of compelling activity and conversation dashboards that display: subscriber counts, unique visitors, page views, length of visit, content popularity, etc.

2.9 Policies

As with the evolution of any new innovation, there is an initial period during which society and users struggle with rules, regulations, policies and procedures. Earlier in this Chapter we outlined for you "How to Conduct Yourself" online and even what the "Rules of Engagement" are.

Creating a set of Policies and Procedures for Social Media is however a very detailed exercise and not covered in this Report. At the time of going to print

Marcie Roggow and Frances Flynn Thorsen were just wrapping up work on a Social Media Policy Manual for the real estate industry.

The manual strives to assist real estate brokers to assess and manage their online risk across property listing sites, blogs, online forums and messaging venues. The manual offers a blueprint for real estate agent and brokers to become partners in a comprehensive risk management initiative to remain compliant.

We recommend that real estate professionals understand the importance to establish an e-policy which determines the best practices and that minimizes risks and maximizes compliance with both state and federal regulations while also adhering to the National Association of REALTORS® Code of Ethics.

For more information visit www.bit.ly/SMPolicy

Chapter 3

Sites & Tools

3.1 Hubs-and-Spokes Framework

The second trend of the 2009 Swanepoel TRENDS Report (retrends.com) introduced the concepts of Outposts and Listening Posts. In the realm of interactive Internet and online communications, finding information, customer reviews and obtaining quality data to improve your business isn't easy. That's why establishing these information Outposts and Listening Posts are keys in your strategy for engaging customers in the places they hang out and where they prefer to build relationships.

Before diving straight into establishing the Outposts and Listening Posts, it is important to setup the Hub-and-Spokes framework to organize the various sites and tools that you may end up using in Social Media.

The sections below will outline the concept and components of the Hub and Outposts of this framework. Chapter 4 will follow with a discussion specific to Listening Posts.

3.2 The Hub

The Hub operates as your central focus in Social Media. It will help in the trust-building objective by giving interested people from any of the Outposts a place where they can get a sense of the "real you." Some real estate professionals may interpret this as being only a website containing marketing messages, a list of residential listings, lead capture forms and other engines from which to enable e-mail drip campaigns. All of these tools add value, but you should also focus on tools that build trust. You will be better served to include a site that is search-engine friendly, easily linkable, highly indexed and frequently updated.

Therefore a blog—or your website with a frequently updated blog attached to it—is a key feature at the Hub of your network. Blogs, if frequently updated with quality information, are highly indexed by search engines and frequently linked to—and shared by—other bloggers and social networkers. As for content that helps you to connect with others, it is one of the best vehicles for indirectly communicating your personal and/or brand characteristics to your visitors in a way that doesn't blatantly shout "do business with me."

3.3 The Outposts

Looking at the big picture, think of the spokes, or Outposts in Social Media, as your way of casting a wide net. Outposts represent culturally distinct networks where you engage potential customers in the places where they prefer to engage others in a conversation online. Suffice it to say, each network is different. In addition to differences in feature sets and their look and feel, each one has a different tone - a unique method or set of expectations amongst its members.

The concept of establishing Outposts can be as simple an idea as staking out a profile and participating in "communities of discussion" on forums such as Facebook, LinkedIn, and Twitter. The more Outposts you're engaged in, the greater amount of exposure you're likely to have, but an important thing to remember is that a hundred Outposts will not make you more effective. It is better to focus on only a few and make sure that the information that passes through them is high in quality.

Your objective: to build genuine trust, credibility and acceptance in each of the Outposts you engage.

3.4 Recommended Strategy

Illustrating the Hub-and-Spokes framework, Outposts and Listening Posts framework (see diagram), consider the center of your influence—the Hub—as the focal point of your online networking activities with all other platforms placed along the periphery like Outposts radiating from the Hub.

Meanwhile, the in-between spaces are populated with blue bubbles. These represent Listening Posts, or

HUB, OUTPOSTS & LISTENING POSTS

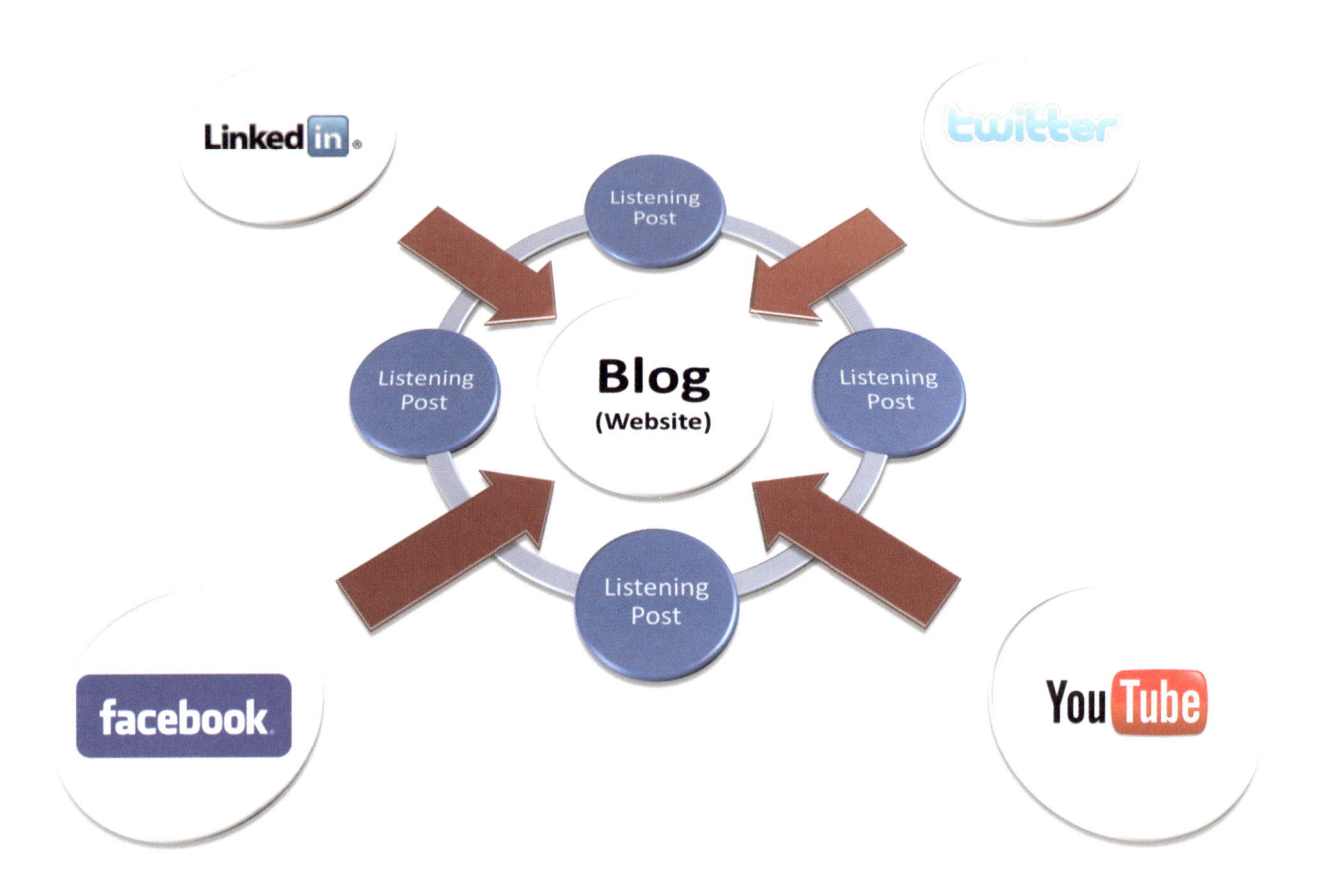

Source: RealSure

extensions, that function as necessary activities that clue you in to the tone, trend and volume of

conversations that relate to you, your brand or niche. This involves such activities as establishing search alerts through the use of online monitoring tools like Google Alerts (google.com/alerts) and RSS feeds and the results page of keyword searches in various communities where your potential customers engage. More about Listening Posts in Chapter 4.

As there are numerous platforms, including blogs, micro-blogs, social networks, discussion forums, video-sharing, photo-sharing and slide-sharing sites available, five were selected to provide real estate professionals the greatest effectiveness.

They Are:
- Your Blog
- Facebook
- Twitter
- LinkedIn
- YouTube

3.5 Your Blog

Your blog should be a platform where you can reveal to the world your personal and professional values, interests and passions. Some might think of this as a curious set of activities that might be akin to self-destruction when it comes to personal privacy. That view isn't surprising. Many definitions given about blogs make comparisons to personal journals or private diaries but that is not necessarily the kind of self-revelation intended here.

Reveal Your Values, Interests and Passions

When you think about marketing your brand, think about how many opportunities there truly are to talk about it at a time when prospective customers are most receptive to hear you. Family, friends and past clients notwithstanding, consider the last time you tried to educate a casual acquaintance, at a party or networking function, about all that you do as a real estate agent.

You can say all you want about your analytical skills, negotiating prowess, philanthropic activities, community leadership, financial acumen, marketing effectiveness and unique value. But, if the Harris Poll (harrispollonline.com) is any indication, then chances are that all others will hear from you is tantamount to: *Blah, blah, blah …car salesman …blah, blah …market analysis …blah …negotiator.*

Typically, the times when people are most receptive about your brand (family, friends and past clients notwithstanding) are those times when they either have need of services similar to yours or when they develop a desire to opt-in to receive more information about you.

But consider this: when members of the public finally act to learn more about you, what will they find? Hopefully, it isn't the marketing slick with the tired old mantra about your commitment to quality services that compel prospective customers to be your client for life; better that they should find clues and insights into your professionalism and core values. An effective way to reveal that information is through a regular stream of writings in a professionally appropriate public journal.

That's the kind of journaling that adds value. Journaling that indirectly introduces the public to you and your business through the values, interests and passions that fills in the spaces between the lines of the helpful articles you publish online. Remember, the more helpful and informative the article, the better it will be received. And, to punctuate your helpfulness, it will be a journal (blog) that publishes much of that information gratis.

With each blog post you'll tend to share your opinions while drawing from your knowledge and observations about the world around you. At times these opinions might reference external sources that will likely include opinions posted by other bloggers. When you do that, what you say about them, how you say it and the respect you give their ideas—or lack thereof—will speak volumes about your character.

Along that line, when your readers stop to post comments about your opinions—whether in agreement with you or not—your treatment of those comments will similarly say loads about you, your negotiating skills, deftness in facilitation, professionalism and respect for others.

It's in all the ways mentioned above that a blog represents the opportunity for you to reveal to the world a hint of your personal and professional values, interests and passions.

Create Conversations. Always try and create dialogue on your blog. The more you share with individuals (with respect to content) the more you will establish your credibility. Allow for public comments and feedback.

Add Features. Add applications and other features that will draw individuals to your blog. Adding polls, videos, or information from other Social Networks will improve the popularity.

> "When it comes to the influence in Social Media, not everyone is high profile. Actually, according to a presentation made to the Library of Congress in June 2008, the majority of YouTube videos are not meant for 'mass media.' In fact, on average, each video was intended for less than 1,000 views."

–Michael Wesch
Kansas State University

Maximizing Your Blog

Posting Articles. Posting new content on your blog is always important as it gives people a reason to read and review what you say. Try posting new articles every couple of days.

Design. Create a compelling and elegant layout including the location of your contact details, information about you, your background, your articles, etc. Remember that the layout should fit your online persona (Chapter 2).

Clutter Free. Blogs are often cluttered with lots of information. Design something that is simple and easy to navigate. Remember, people have come to your blog to read what you wrote, so make sure that they can get to posts and articles quickly and without hassle.

3.6 Facebook

The crème de la Crème of Social Networking sites is Facebook. Since its launch it has exploded into the lead with over 250 million members. After gaining a large following at Harvard it expanded its services to other college campuses and high schools all across the U.S. It eventually grew to include anyone above the age of 13. Of its 250 million worldwide users it is estimated that some 42 million are in the U.S. According to Hitwise, and with its 2009 acquisition of Friendfeed, Facebook solidified its rank as the #1 Social Networking site holding 39% of all social networking traffic.

The Culture

Facebook's network culture tends to be less formal and is similar to say a backyard barbecue. It's important to remember that "less formal" doesn't mean unduly casual or overly familiar. There are many stories of chagrined college graduates losing out on job opportunities as a result of beer-binging photo journals they unfortunately decided to post on their Facebook profile. Instead, when you think of the "less formal" nature of Facebook, imagine a barbecue you host in your backyard where the invited guests are past clients or future customers. Everyone is free to wear shorts and relax, but keep the dialog at a business casual level.

Profiles and Pages

So how does the framework of Facebook set itself apart from the rest? First it's important to take a look at how it categorizes individuals. When creating a profile on Facebook you have two options - *a Personal Profile or a Fan Page.*

A *Personal Profile* is a profile that is designed around you. Capped at 5,000 friends (or connections), this profile allows you to: upload photos and sort them into albums, upload videos, fill out information about you, share links, share notes and share your preferences. You are also able to view all the *Personal Profiles* of any of your friends and anything they post.

A *Fan Page* is a profile page typically designed around a brand, product, business, service, celebrity or public figure. Unlike Personal Profiles, *Fan Pages* can have over 5,000 connections; commonly known as fans. As these pages cater more toward a business approach they include all the capabilities of a standard page with the addition of insights, or information regarding your post quality and interactions on your *Fan Page*. The limitation of a *Fan Page* is that your interaction with everyone is limited to only the page you created; you are not able to view the profiles of your connections like you would if you were using a *Personal Profile*.

So which is more suitable, a *Personal Profile* or a *Fan Page*?

It depends on your purpose (Chapter 2) for joining Facebook. If your intent is to share stories, photos and events with family and friends or a close group of business partners and clients, then a *Personal Profile* is probably the better choice. If your goal is to offer services to a very large group of people then you should consider a *Fan Page*. Just remember, it's considerably more difficult to build up your connections with a *Fan Page* than with a *Personal Profile*.

Ways to Communicate

Facebook is home to a large variety of features, the majority of which are accessible regardless of the type of profile you choose. Most of the features are tied to the profiles themselves, including the standard features that appear as tabs at the top of a *Personal Profile* or *Fan Page* - Wall, Info, Photos, and Video.

Chapter 3 | Sites and Tools

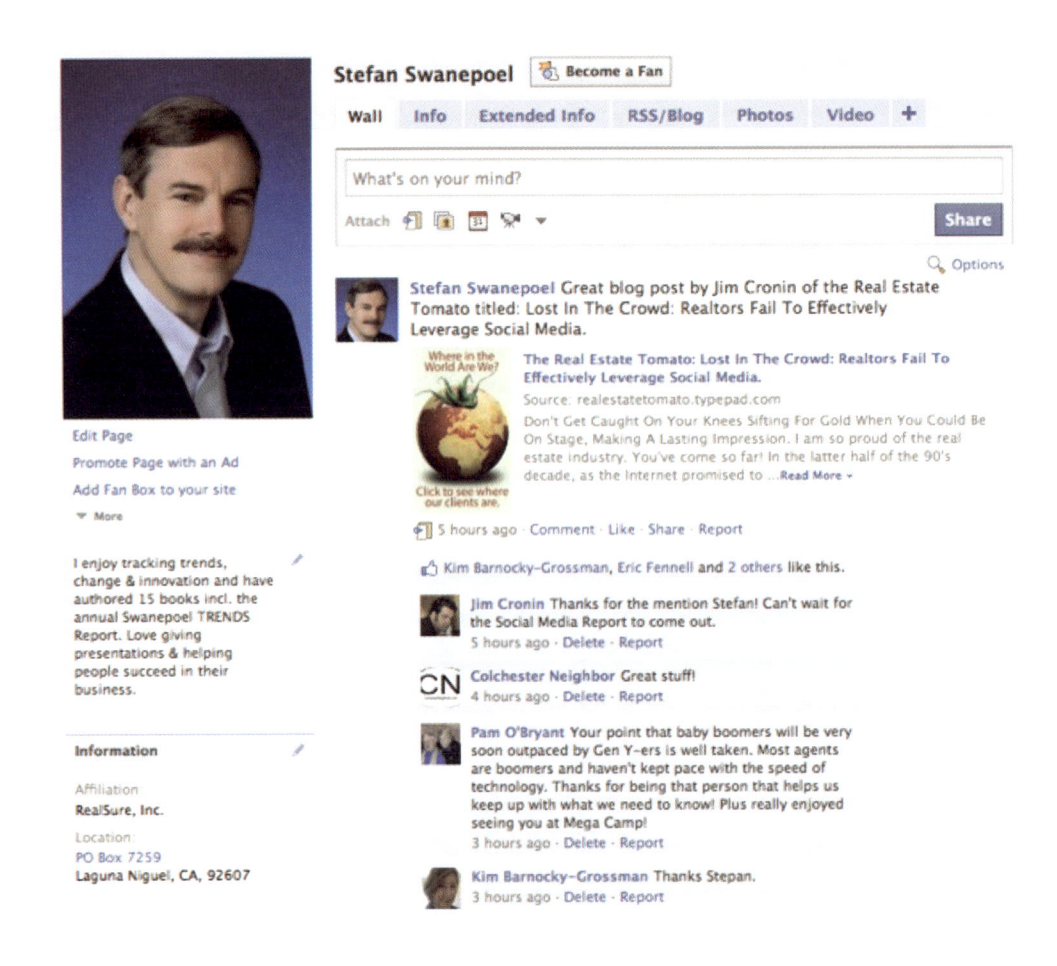

Example of Fan Page for Stefan Swanepoel

The *Wall* feature is the most popular method of communication on Facebook. Consider it as a blog where you can post articles, stories, ideas, questions, comments, pictures, or links. However, unlike a blog that only allows the user to post content, the *Wall* also allows anyone else, whether a friend (for a *Personal Profile*) or a fan (for a *Fan Page*), to post on it. With that the *Wall* becomes a place for dialog and discussion. Individuals can comment on a particular post (which acts as a reply) or just send you a new message.

The *Groups* feature is another method of communicating on Facebook. This feature allows individuals to organize groups or communities around organizations, causes, etc. Although an integral feature in Facebook, in recent years Groups have been overshadowed by the creation of *Fan Pages*, and as a result, are now viewed as intimate communities.

The *Info*, Photos and Video features, which each operate within their own tab on a profile page (*Personal Profile* or *Fan Page*), are additional methods in which you can share information about who you are. The *Info* tab supplies a quick summary of who you are and the Photos tab supplies all your photos, whether posted by you or by others that have you tagged in them. The *Video* feature acts in a similar fashion to the *Photos* tab.

Above the features seen on profiles, Facebook also welcomes users (every time they log on) to the *Newsfeed* feature. The *Newsfeed* feature operates as a central location for all of the "news" or activity that's going on in Facebook. This includes everything from pictures a friend posted from a trip to Hawaii to the article they posted regarding some changes in Social Media. Anything that occurs on the profiles of your friends—or wherever you've elected to become a fan—

is then sent to your *Newsfeed*. On the reverse side, this is a great marketing tool as it gives you exposure to all of your connections.

Beyond the standard features that everyone is given such as the *Wall* and *Newsfeed*, Facebook also allows for some customization through the additions of applications; Apps (facebook.com/apps). Apps range from games to calendars; movies to the marketplace; RSS feeds to testimonials; and there are even Apps that allow you to retrieve content from other Social Media sites. Depending upon the settings of the App, it will either be placed, as its own unique tab at the top of your profile, or it will be listed underneath a tab called Boxes that operates as a collection point for Apps. Here are some Facebook Apps to consider for your profile: Discussion Boards, Social RSS and Friend Me Up!

increase the opportunity for others to examine your credibility and who you are as a person. The more you share with individuals (with respect to content) the greater the odds of success. But every now and then, take some time (if using a personal profile) to write on other people's Walls and start discussions that way.

Add Sources. When using your Wall, add information from other sources like Twitter, YouTube or an article that you wrote or found interesting. A larger variety of relevant content brings credibility to your profile.

Add a Personal Touch. Social Media and Facebook are all about connecting to people, so add a personal touch like a few photos or videos. Share what's important, but check first to ensure it fits with the online persona that you're trying to establish. This includes a complete and detailed profile page, or creating a profile badge.

DID YOU KNOW!

A new page on Facebook—FacebookForGood—is rapidly becoming a popular place for individuals to share the positive influence that Facebook has made in their lives. Lined with stories including "Missing Nepali ski racer found via Facebook" and "UK teenager saved by Facebook," it is a place for individuals to connect and share stories. However, the power of Facebook stems from networking campaigns and friends communicating with friends. Often revolved around groups such as Barack Obama (One Million Strong for Barack) used for the 2008 Presidential Elections or "Save Darfur," Facebook has been able to unite individuals around a common purpose.

Maximizing Facebook

There are many ways to optimize your Facebook; here are a few to get more people to notice you.

Update your Status. Posting new content on your Wall freshens up the look and the feel of your page.
Create Conversations. Always try and create dialogue on your page. More interactions on your profile

Use Apps. Apps are a good way of adding variety to your page. Select a few apps that are relevant and useful, and avoid adding those that can cause a distraction from your message or brand.

Partake in Groups. Whether you join a group, or create your own, participate in them actively by discussing ideas, events or posting on the Wall.

Host Events. Regardless if you host an online event or at a physical location, events are a great way of connecting people and bringing Facebook to life. Invite people, but remember to stay focused on who you're inviting. There is no point in inviting men to bridal showers or women to bachelor parties.

Conduct Polls. Polls are a good way of determining what individuals, or groups of individuals think.

Become a Fan. Follow influential people by becoming a fan in your industry/market and contribute to their page. It's a great way to stay updated and a good place to ask questions.

Add an Ad. Create a Facebook ad for your target market. It's a simple way that gets you to market yourself to specific people or groups.

3.7 LinkedIn

LinkedIn is primarily a professional network with the ability for users to maintain an online resume and reach out to other professionals they would like to keep contact with. Since its launch it has grown to include 45 million users in over 200 countries. With one person joining every second, 80% of companies now turn to LinkedIn as a primary resource to find employees.

The Culture

View the LinkedIn network culture as the formal business meeting. LinkedIn caters to a user-base of business professionals. As such, the culture tends to be more formal with some users opting to reserve statements, updates and information sharing to those having a strictly professional tone.

Online Resume

Designed around business relations and a contact network, LinkedIn operates primarily as a network of Online Resumes. Its contact network is constructed from people you know (direct connection), the people your contacts know (second-degree connection) and all the contacts of those second-degree contacts (third-degree connection). To connect with anyone, LinkedIn requires a pre-existing relationship or contact introduction. By operating this way, LinkedIn allows users to build trust, strengthen relationships, or enhance visibility with customers and prospects. The platform offers various features and services to expand your resume and establish your credibility, including *Recommendations, Answers, Search Groups* and *Applications*.

Features

Recommendations is one of the most prominent, simple and great features to use in order to build your credibility. As the name suggests, LinkedIn allows users to recommend one another, much like testimonials. An individual can request a recommendation or it can be offered freely.

Answers is one of the more powerful features on LinkedIn—for both those asking questions and as those providing answers. The opportunity for you to help someone by answering his or her question is powerful in itself. Additionally, every answer has the opportunity to be selected as a "best answer" by those posting questions. When selected, LinkedIn updates your profile (see screenshot) to reflect this fact, which further works to the benefit of your trust-building efforts.

Search Groups offers similar benefits as *Answers*, but within a focused niche. You can find almost any group matching your interests by simply selecting *Search Groups* from the pick list at the top of your LinkedIn page and then typing keywords that represent your areas of interest. By Summer 2009, *Search Groups* operated a list of at over 70 groups related to the keywords *real estate referral*.

Applications, much like apps on any Social Media platform allow a user to customize and express themselves, much like printing a resume on a certain type of paper or using special trimmings. It application help to close an online expression-ability gap. It applications let you express yourself in a variety of ways including, sharing your most recent blog articles, showing a presentation, sharing files, presenting a list of recommended books, etc.

Maximizing LinkedIn

Updates. Post new content on LinkedIn. It refreshes the look and the feel of your page. New content gives people a reason to look at your page.

Jobs. Use job search if you're looking for a job, but also use it to help others find one. By helping others you add value to your profile on LinkedIn.

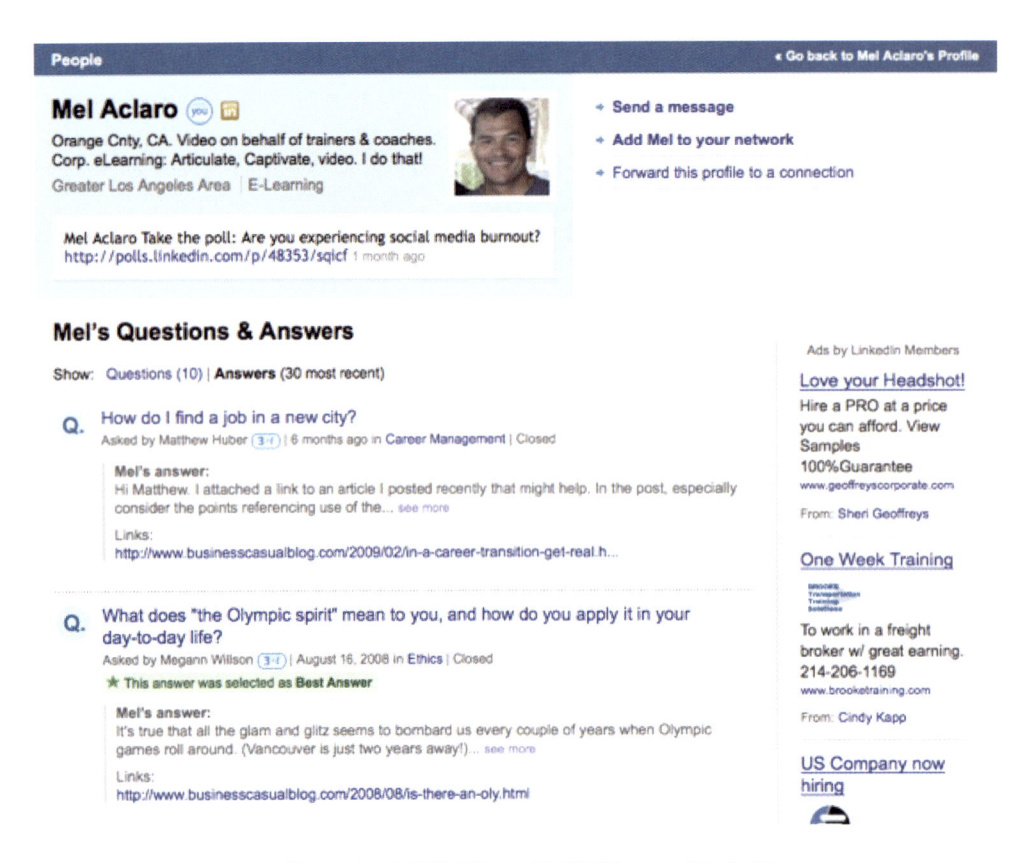

Example of Q&A Page of Mel Aclaro on LinkedIn

Questions and Answers. Answers, the Groups you're affiliated with, the types of discussions you engage in, the manner in which you engage others in discussion and any other history or expression of help you can offer.

Integrate Applications. Adding applications to your online resume allows you to add a personal touch, whether it is adding a blog-based application or a photo sharing application.

Recommend. Recommendations offer an easy way to spread influence and to improve networking. By supplying testimonials you increase the value of other individual's resumes. Make sure you also get recommended.

Add Details. Add previous companies, schools and alumni associations. By filling out as much detail to your online resume, you expand the ways that individuals can connect with you.

Search. Beyond any standard searching, actively search for people to connect with based on location, company name, school name and interests, etc.

Groups. Joining groups is a valuable tool, particularly on LinkedIn. It is a great way for individuals to stay connected, but more importantly, it offers large networking opportunities. For example, real estate professionals might also consider joining groups with Virtual Assistants, Home Stagers or lawyers to gain access to those contact networks.

Create Connections. Share with individuals your network of contacts, be willing to make introductions. Be wise about it, and make sure that your network stays valuable by avoiding connections with people that you do not care about.

Introductions. Make introductions for people, if you value both parties and you believe that creating a connection won't hurt you in anyway, it's a good way to expand networks and help others.

3.8 Twitter

Although launched in 2006, Twitter a mircoblogging site that revolves around tweets, really exploded in 2008 and according to HubSpot (hubspot.com), 70% of all Twitter users to that point signed up during that year. Nielson estimates that between February 08 and February 09 Twitter grew by 1382 percent and according to eMarketer (emarketer.com), 54% of all Fortune 1,000 companies are active on Twitter.

The Culture

It's a cocktail party. As with a live cocktail party you'll likely find a lot of people milling about engaged in small talk. Many of the attendees may or may not know each other personally or professionally. It's a place where you should "walk around" while engaging in easy banter until you find a conversation that's more deeply engaging. With these deeper connections you might suggest follow-up meetings in a different venue where you can learn more about each other's interests. *Hint—suggest a mutual connection on LinkedIn or Facebook.*

> **"By using Twitter as a means of networked protest, it has become a window to the world."**
>
> *-Unkown*

Often described as the SMS of the internet, limiting its Tweets to 140 characters, Twitter has quickly risen into the top five of the most visited Social Networking Sites with over 25 million users at the time of this Report. Most of Twitter's success comes from its simple, easy and quick communication capabilities.

Their website states that:

Twitter is a service for friends, family and co-workers to communicate and stay connected through the exchange of quick, frequent answers to one simple question: What are you doing?

Many people therefore use Twitter as a type of social chat forum. However, during the past year a shift among many users began to take place and Twitter has also become a vehicle to rapidly distribute news, events and quality information to a large base of followers. For example, we use Twitter regularly to share changes, strategies, trends and news occurring in the real estate industry with friends and followers (see screenshot).

Ways to Communicate

To limit Twitter as a simple chat platform would be incorrect. As each Twitter user is connected to, on average, a few hundred other Twitter users, the platform exponentially explodes the "simple chat" into a "huge conversation" with literally thousands and thousands of people beyond the original user's immediate connection.

There are hundreds of URL shortening services/sites. Here is a list of 10 of the most well known.

- tinyurl.com
- budurl.com
- snipurl.com
- bit.ly
- is.gd
- ow.ly
- cli.gs
- u.nu
- poprl.com
- zi.ma

Chapter 3 | Sites and Tools

Example of Stefan Swanepoel Twitter Account

Therefore, one of Twitter's direct benefits resides in your *network influence*. That is, your ability to enable others with whom you are connected to take some sort of action through their extended network. Upon receiving one of your posts (tweet) your connections can decide if they want to re-post (retweet) your message to their network. The bigger their network the more potential there will be for other people to see your message.

So why join Twitter? There is no doubt that by 2008/9 the concept of Microblogging had moved mainstream with Twitter leading the charge. This was not only validated by President Obama's use of Twitter during his presidential campaign, but also by the frequent use and reference to Twitter on CNN, The New York Times and other mainstream media outlets. However, Twitter benefits go beyond following the top trends or current news and events. It also allows you to optimize your rankings and market your brand. Here are some recommended practices to explore:

Hashtags

One popular feature among Twitter users is the use of hashtags (#). Hashtagging is a way to group related tweets posted by different Twitter users together in one group. Twitter users need not be related to each other via network connections in order to see each other's tweets via hashtag grouping.

It is used in a tweet by adding a Twitter #hashtag such as #FridayFollow to your post. The trick is in knowing which keywords others are using for purposes of grouping related conversations. For this reason, before using a hashtag, we recommend the following:

Identifying hashtags. Use Tagalus (http://tagal.us) a dictionary for hashtags to find a list of thousands of hashtags as defined by other users.

Tracking hashtags. To track tweets with hashtag in real-time use Twitterfall (twitterfall.com) or to receive alerts on used hashtags try Twilert (twilert.com)

Using hashtags. Be careful not too overuse hashtags and that the usage thereof adds or is applicable to the discussion.

Maximizing Twitter

Create. Create a profile that explains who you are. Make sure that you include a customized background that is simple and easy to see and read.

Provide. Provide quality posts and information.

Be Courteous. Respond in a timely manner to @ and DM messages. This also includes using auto-responding tools, and auto-tweets; there is a right time and place for them.

Add Connections. Follow Twitterers with similar interests. Also make sure that a lot of people follow you. Twitter ranks users using an algorithm that compares these two values among others.

Be Active. Learn to participate in conversations with other Twitterers. This includes asking questions and providing feedback on re-tweet (RT) posts.

Clear is Key. Be transparent, sincere and respectful of others.

Quality. Do not post inappropriate comments that are harmful in anyway.

Don't Sell. Do not constantly sell your products or services.

Simplify. Integrate Twitter posts with all your other Social Media sites and activities.

Time Tweets. Avoid sending out a barrage of tweets all at once. Spread them out throughout the day. No one enjoys receiving tweet-spam from a tweeterbox.

3.9 YouTube

Founded in early 2005, YouTube is the third most popular Social Networking site, the leader in online video and the second largest search engine. YouTube operates as an online video-sharing site where users can share stories, music videos and comments. With over 100 million viewers watching more that 6.3 billion videos, YouTube holds the attention of approximately 42% of the online video viewing market with approximately 62.6 videos per viewer according to comScore. According to Wikipedia, before the launch of YouTube in 2005 there were few simple methods available for ordinary computer users who wanted to post videos online. YouTube has made it easy for anyone to post videos online and share them with friends and family. It attracts individuals of all ages and backgrounds by offering visitors a wide range of content from instructional to entertainment.

The Culture

It's an interesting mishmash. YouTube has professional video content juxtaposed with other topics ranging from moderately informal to outright foolish and inappropriate. One way to think of YouTube is to consider it as a video shelf where you place your own video collection, one that you will choose to occasionally share with others who take you up on your barbecue invitation or business meeting borrowing from the Facebook and LinkedIn metaphors. The collection might include topics ranging from personal commentaries on professionally appropriate subject matter to formal business presentations. It may even include "how-to" tutorials and property listing videos.

Channel Yourself

When you join YouTube, you end up creating a profile, or YouTube Channel. It's a centralized place where anyone can see your public videos, favorites, comments, subscribers, video log, bulletin status, and recent activity. Users can also see statistics including: membership status, website information, etc. User profiles are designed with customizability in mind and use a modular design in the features layout within an individual channel. As such, users can customize channels to fit their own needs.

Features

Video-showcasing is the addition of productions created by others that you admire or find valuable. These others might include sharing YouTube videos produced and shared by professional speakers, trainers and other personalities. It's okay, too, to reserve a section in your YouTube channel for any property videos you professionally produce for marketing your listings.

DID YOU KNOW!

YouTube's most viewed video, Evolution of Dance, is a 6-minute video with over 120 million views (Wikipedia, 2009). To put this into perspective, Superbowl 2008 had nearly 96 million viewers and one 30-second ad cost $3 million. That means it would have cost $36 million if that video had been aired during the Superbowl; even then it would have had 24 million less viewers.

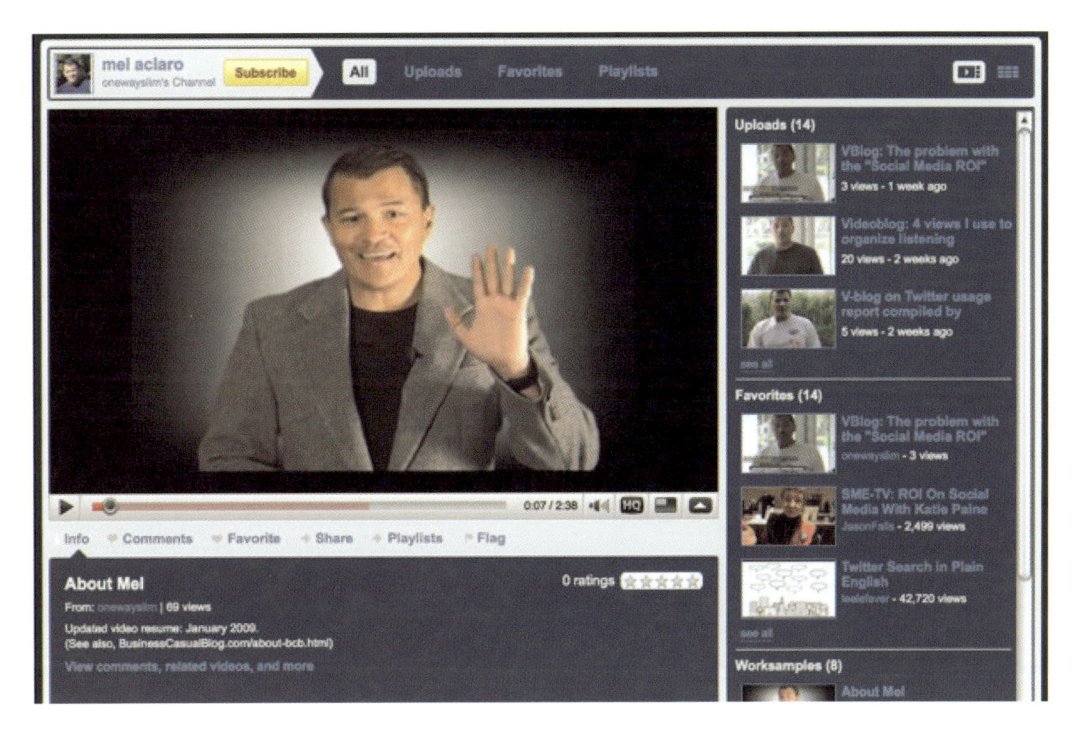

Example of Mel Aclaro YouTube Channel

Favorites. Adding video, created by another YouTube user, to your channel is as simple as selecting "Favorite" at the bottom of any YouTube video.

Maximizing YouTube

Create. Create a channel that explains who you are. Make sure that you include a customized background and simple layout that is easy to see and read. Make sure that it is branded visually.

Provide. Social Media, and in particular, YouTube, is focused around a value add philosophy. Videos can gain popularity through their value. Value can be anything from content rich videos to comedic skits.

Socialize The Channel. Respond to people who post questions or comments. Make it easy on yourself and post a video response. Use the community and address your videos to a specific people/groups, i.e. "Good Afternoon Internet." Add Subscriptions. Link to other channels that you find valuable and create a network.

Seek Subscribers. Like fans or followers, subscribers are people that want to hear what you say. A fast way to gain subscribers is to do video responses to other videos.

Ratings. Ratings are the key to popularity on YouTube, the more ratings and views, the more prominent the video. Recommend to people to rate the video after they see it.

Sidebar. Fill out the sidebar, or description information, for each video. If you end up talking about articles or other sites, or even listings, add a link so that people can do more research by themselves.

Annotations. YouTube allows you to add annotations to videos, be careful when working with these. It is okay to add one or possibly two during a video at strategic locations. Any more than that and they become distracting.

Tags. Use tags, or keywords, to optimize your video so that it can be found easily.

Keep it Short. Majority of videos are between 3-5 minutes with an average length of two minutes.

Chapter 4

Monitoring the Conversation

4.1 Components of Listening Posts

Staying in touch with an information base that is growing exponentially is crucial. And with each passing day it is vital that your blogging activities and Social Media interactions remain current and relevant in order to attract the attention of others. As this happens—assuming you write compelling and interesting content about your niche interests and expertise—others will want to link to your articles and, spurred by your articles, piggy-back their thoughts with yours on their own blog posts and online activities. And there will be others that are content to just post comments or simply share links to your article or blog site.

monitoring the conversation are:

- Conversation discovery
- Conversation aggregation
- Conversation escalation
- Conversation participation
- Conversation tracking

Listening Posts differ from the traditional feedback tools like focus groups, interviews, surveys and polls. They're different in the sense that Listening Posts give us clues about the online conversations that are happening around us now. If what is being said is positive, you'll have an opportunity to say thank you.

> **DID YOU KNOW!**
>
> Recent studies have shown that of the estimated 3.5 billion word-of-mouth conversations that occur around the world each day, approximately 2.3 billion of them—roughly 2/3—make a reference to a brand, product or service. Word of mouth is increasingly manifesting itself through digital Social Media, where it spreads both farther and faster.

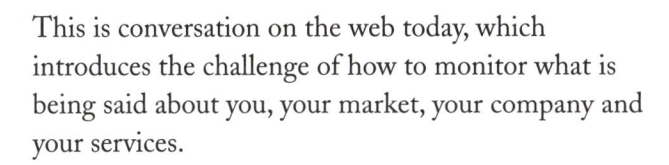

This is conversation on the web today, which introduces the challenge of how to monitor what is being said about you, your market, your company and your services.

The Hubs-and-Spokes Chapter 3 concept and the blue bubbles gracing the space between the Hub and the Outposts (in the diagram) were identified as Listening Posts—online tools supported by automation services. Some can be as simple as the use of search engines and keyword alerts, while others may be as sophisticated as customized third-party "dashboards" for which it may make sense to pay a nominal fee as your business grows.

According to a marketech report by Marketing Savant (marketingsavant.com), the best practices for

If negative, you'll have an opportunity to rebut, frame proper context or, if warranted, publicly apologize in a professional manner while having an opportunity with the last word to explain how you will ensure the experience is more positive moving forward. But, even if the conversation isn't about you at all—perhaps it's about trends in the industry or events in one of your farm areas—you'll have an opportunity to give guidance and offer expertise. In other words, Listening Posts help you be aware, relevant and a player.

What you want are online engines working for you to trigger alerts or filter views based on keywords or phrases that give clues to the industry, trends, customer perceptions, competitor behavior, technologies, politics etc.

Chapter 4 | Monitoring the Conversation

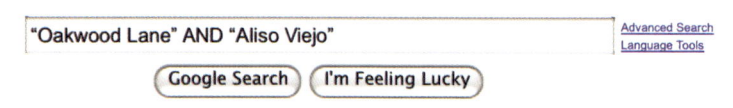

Example of a Manual Query

Specific Keywords to Track

- Your company/personal name
- Your competitor's company/personal name
- Products/Services/Brands/Trademarks
- Key customers/potential customers
- Key markets you operate in or wish to operate in

What Online Media to Track

- Search Engine Results
- Press Releases
- News Services/Group
- Blogs
- Social Networks
- Video Releases
- Podcasts
- Resource sites such as Wikipedia
- Q & A sites such as Yahoo Answers

Buzz Monitoring Tools

Marketing Savant also provides an excellent list of Listening Posts described as their "buzz monitoring tools." Here are some good ones from their list:

- Google or Yahoo Alerts
- Google Blog/Web Search
- Google Reader
- Google Trends or Trendrr
- Friendfeed
- Technorati
- FeedRinse
- BlogPulse
- Backtype
- Filtrbox.com

4.2 Manual Queries

Manual queries are a valuable but often forgotten tool when trying to track relevant conversations. Let's consider the fictitious case of Jane Smith. Jane is a real estate agent specializing in the residential real estate market in and around Aliso Viejo, California. She has a keen interest in knowing whenever her name or her business is mentioned on any blog, microblog, discussion forum or social network. As far as that goes, she should conduct periodic searches in her favorite search engine using her name or her business name as keywords.

But, if that were as far as Jane went she'd be limiting herself to a reactive state. That is, she gets to participate in online conversations only after the fact.

Better late than never. But she should also consider keywords that help her to maintain more pro-active opportunities for dialog. Here are a few illustrative suggestions:

- **"Oakwood Lane" AND "Aliso Viejo"**—This might represent the street name and town in which she recently signed a new listing. It will help her to know whether—and where in the online social sphere—anyone might be discussing or blogging about any of the properties on that street. By the same token she might also consider queries that include the name of the specific development or planned community.

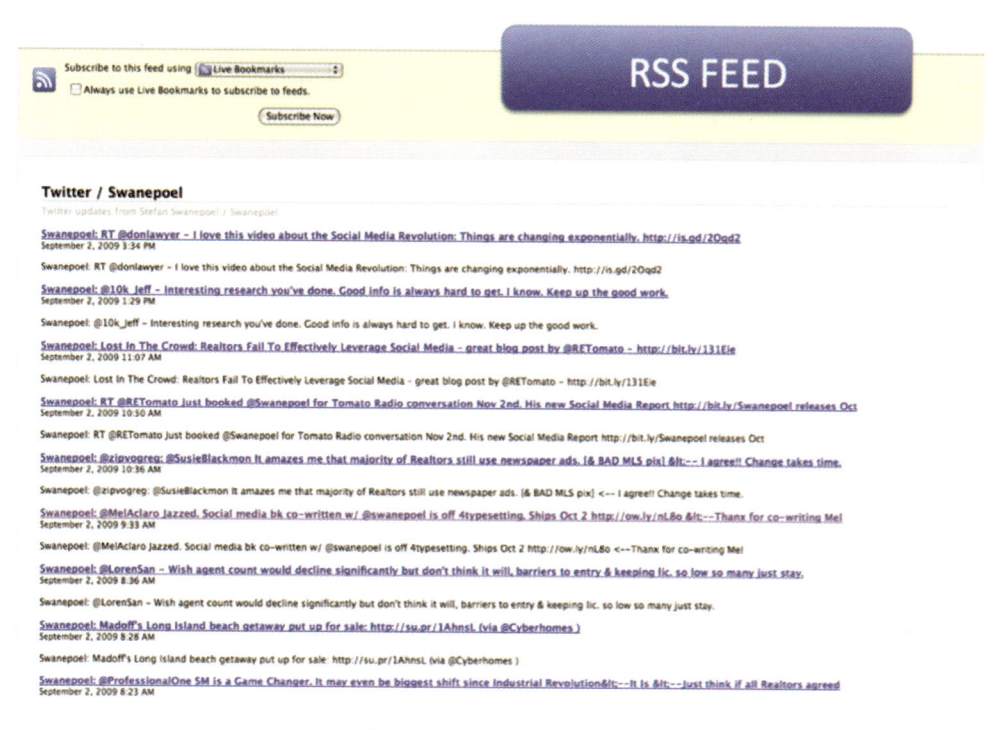

Example of an RSS Feed

- **"Imperial Highway" AND (development OR construction)**—This illustrates an example query to receive any updates she should be aware of regarding a construction project affecting this major intersection in her farm. Any updates that turn up would be good information to post on her blog and/or in her farming newsletters.

- **"Short sale" AND (DRE OR "Department of Real Estate" OR legislation) AND "Aliso Viejo"**— This illustrates an example keyword search that might alert her to any politically- or regulatory-related discussions about the short sale market in her farming area.

These are just a few examples of listening/awareness queries using a manually initiated online search. But, if this is the extent of Jane's listening activities she would be very busy indeed, conducting manual searches all day long. Jane would be more efficient to centralize much of this information on just one or two sites, or establish automatic triggers that alert her via email whenever some of these queries play out in the social web.

4.3 RSS Feeds

An acronym for Really Simple Syndication (also known as Rich Site Summary), RSS is a way for publishers of web content to circulate updates of their information via a special page called an RSS feed. The term RSS feed is also used interchangeably with the page's associated web address.

You can elect to subscribe to a publisher's RSS feed by using special software called a feed reader (also known as an RSS reader or news reader). There are many free options for RSS readers available. A few popular online services include:

- Google Reader (google.com/reader)
- NetNewsWire (newsgator.com/netnewswire)
- FeedDemon (feeddemon.com)
- Netvibes (netvibes.com)
- Pageflakes (pageflakes.com)

By taking the RSS feed (the address portion) from websites that elect to syndicate content and placing it into your feed reader you will streamline one form of listening activity by having created a free account from which you can view new updates; potentially, from multiple sites at the same time.

The beauty of this arrangement is in the ability you have to quickly scan only new information with each visit. RSS feed readers allow you to mark articles and updates that you have previously read. Once marked as having been read, those articles no longer appear during future visits to your feed reader. This allows you to more efficiently allocate your time to scanning and reading only relevant content.

> "RSS feeds change not only the metric, but the information you're looking for."
>
> *-Jason Falls*
> Social Media Explorer

Notice that, in addition to blogs and news sites, some search engines also make RSS feeds available for the results page of your search queries. You can collect some of the manual inquiries such as @Swanepoel on Twitter (see screenshot).

As you scan titles from your RSS feeds, be especially cognizant of articles or discussions where it would make sense for you to comment, share a link with your other network contacts or write a blog article. The blog article could, in turn, be shared through your network contacts on Twitter, LinkedIn, Facebook or YouTube.

4.4 Google Alerts

Google Alerts (google.com/alerts) is another simple (free) online listening tool that allows you to set up keywords about which you will be informed via email whenever those keywords appear in websites, blogs or Google discussion forums. The various types of web content for which you can set up alerts include:

- **News alerts.** Inform you of the latest articles from Google news search that contain your keywords.

- **Web alerts.** Inform you of the latest web pages from the top twenty results of a Google web search containing your keywords.

- **Blog alerts.** Inform you of the latest blog posts from the top ten results of a Google blog search containing your keywords.

- **Comprehensive alerts.** Combine results from News, Web and Blog searches into a single email alert.

- **Video alerts.** Inform you of the top ten results from a Google video search containing your keywords.

- **Group alerts.** An email that aggregates new posts containing your keywords that appears in the top fifty results of a search in Google groups.

As in all listening activities, you will want to scan the titles emailed to you by the alert system and consider conversations and articles where it will benefit you to comment, share a link or write an article on your blog. These can then be shared through your Outposts on Twitter, LinkedIn, Facebook or YouTube.

> "Setting up "digital listening posts" is essential to help learn about not just the good things people are saying about you, but the bad things as well. Getting an early "heads up" can make all the difference in the world between crisis and total disaster."
>
> *-Aliza Sherman*
> Web Worker Daily

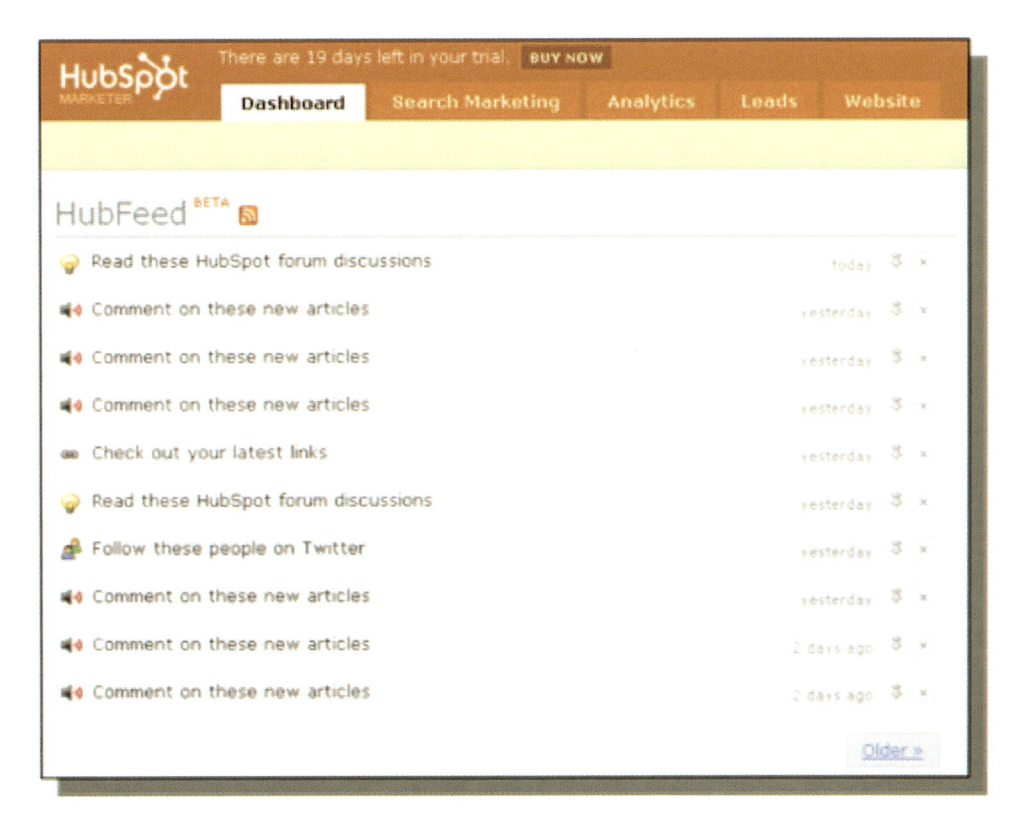

Example of a Monitoring Service

4.5 Message Board Alerts

BoardReader (boardreader.com) is another free listening tool that allows you to search for occurrences of certain keywords across message boards and discussion forums. Similar to Google Alerts, you can schedule alerts to be delivered via email. But, with BoardReader you also have the option of subscribing to search results via RSS.

In addition to the obvious keywords such as those related to: your name, your business name and the terms: "realtor" and "real estate agent," you should also consider adding keywords for counties, cities, subdivisions and communities that you farm, as well as those related to the names of competitors and niche services (1031; short sales; home staging; finding a Realtor®; etc.).

Add also any other services or interests for which you have developed a specialty and feel you can speak with some authority. When alerts arrive with related titles, go to those sites by clicking the link provided in the alert or RSS feed and consider where it would be appropriate to join the conversation.

> "Listening to the buzz around your brand is not only important from a reputation management standpoint, but also because it serves as a way to better understand ways of improving your brand."
>
> *-Nick Christensen*
> Social Media Trader

WHY SOCIAL MEDIA IS YOUR FUTURE SEO STRATEGY

Source: Adam Singer
The Future Buzz

Cycle of how social supports SEO

- Start: Quality content gets published
- Content gets editorial shares, links
- Site gains subscribers
- Thriving community supporting site grows
- Site receives digital PR from niche as by-product of community
- Reputation is reinforced as referential, authoritative brand for the niche
- Site gains authority in the engines
- Sustainable stream of users discover site organically

4.6 Paid Monitoring Services

Up to now the focus has been on free services to help you monitor online discussions that affect you or your brand in some way. These are great when you're starting off and are still getting your feet wet with Social Media and online engagement, but it is also advisable in the startup phase to avoid immediately outlaying funds for monitoring services while you're still coming up to speed with your Hubs-and-Spokes strategy. But, over time, as your diligence and efficiencies pay off, as more people visit the Hub that is your blog and website, and as your business or brokerage continues to grow, it will make sense for you to consider one of the many paid monitoring services.

The pricing for such services can vary from a few hundred dollars a month to a few thousand dollars per year. In addition to the convenience of having a one-stop dashboard that gives quantitative and graphical representations of the occurrences of keywords, you're also given the benefit of insight about your competitors, as well as information about your online influence.

Online influence is an interesting new metric that is being refined daily. It's typically recorded through metrics about the actions others have taken relative to your online activities. For example, services such as Hubspot (hubspot.com) make it a point to include metrics about the number of times your blog or Twitter posts were viewed, how many times they were shared with others, which articles on your blog received the most visits, which ones were shared most often, etc. Such dashboards can also include information about who is taking action relative to your Social Media content, where the most activity is occurring and recommendations about which discussions you should read or comment on. An illustration of this was given in an earlier section.

Other monitoring services, such as that provided by Radian6 (radian6.com) also boast the ability to conduct real-time monitoring of discussions about your brand on millions of blog posts, videos, photos, forums, online news and microblogs like Twitter. As your business and team grows you might also opt to take advantage of workflow capabilities. These features allow you to manage real-time responses by assigning them to members of your team, prioritize and categorize online conversations related to your brand or niche while also creating new contacts and/or leads from the online conversations you're presented with.

4.7 Social Media Optimization

As the methods for monitoring conversations evolve, the influence of technology over Social Media will only become stronger as the integration and link between Search Engines and Social Media platforms grow. It is time to realize that Search Engine Optimization (SEO) now includes Social Media Optimization (SMO).

In Cycle of How Social Supports SEO, creator Adam Singer (thefuturebuzz.com) shows how the link between Search Engines and Social Media only becomes stronger as both innovate and integrate together.

Here are a few points to keep in mind as the integration of Search and Social Media becomes stronger.

Algorithms. The algorithms used by search engines are changing, growing and evolving. This means that Search Engines are becoming smarter and more capable of distinguishing organic content from automated content. As this happens remember that organic content has higher value.

> "Search feeds social and social feeds search, there is no mistaking this. Enable success from both directions to feed the other and your returns will steadily increase over time."
>
> *-Nick Christensen*
> Social Media Trader

Content and Updates. When it comes to SEO or SMO, websites that have more updates and good content are read more often naturally become more popular and higher ranked.

Sustainability. Popular sites, networks, blogs, brands or pages are popular for a reason, success is self-reinforcing. A positive reputation as an honest and valuable contributor builds upon itself over time and results in an increase in links and attention at exponential returns. Beyond that, it also supplies new ideas and new content.

When you get down to the basics, SEO and SMO are linked and the connection is getting stronger.

Chapter 5

Tying It All Together

5.1 Dividing Up the Social Media Orchestra

Communicating and marketing with your customers, or potential customers used to be simple. You had a few options such as TV, radio, print, etc. The advent of the Internet and the recent growth of Social Media have in some respect made this process easier, but at the same time considerably more complex as the number of technology, web and online tools has exploded.

Managing the diverse and expanding facets of Social Media can be compared to managing all the components of an orchestra. In the same way that an orchestra consists of different parts—percussion instruments, keyboard, strings, brass, etc.—so Social Media consists of different parts—Blogging, Microblogging, Networks, Wikis, etc.

In both cases the musical instruments or the different components of Social Media can all work autonomously; and successfully so. However, the full sound, power and impact of an orchestra only occur when the conductor enables all of the orchestra members to play together in harmony. The same principle applies to Social Media.

To coordinate all the participants to each play the correct instrument at the right time requires a conductor that uses a music score (a plan) as a guide to direct him when each instrument should be played.

In that same way, view yourself as the conductor of your own Social Media Orchestra. You need not use—or be on—every single Social Media site, but the more of them that you use the more robust and impacting the result will be. However, similar to the music conductor, you must use your Social Media sites (think instruments) harmoniously and with a specific plan (think song/tune) in mind. If you don't, your result will create a less attractive result (think noise).

SUCCESS STORY

Shannon Rountree's search for a new home took an unusual turn when a real estate agent she'd never met (Alison Creamer) added her as a friend on Facebook. Within minutes of accepting the request, Rountree was clicking through photos of Creamer's family, reading about her hobbies and watching home videos of her two golden retrievers. Over the next few days, the two women sent messages back and forth discussing various homes for sale and benefits of several neighborhoods, while Creamer touted her friendly nature and no-pressure sales technique. "In the eight years I've been working, I've only had two or three people ask me about my experience," said Creamer, 37. "Everyone else wants to know if I can relate to them. Can I engage them? These Web sites are kind of like a resume for someone's personality."

Weeks after Creamer "friended" both Shannon Rountree and her husband, John, the couple signed a contract on a three-bedroom, 2,500-square-foot home in Chesapeake's Riverwalk neighborhood for $310,000. "I'm a people person," Rountree said. "And it was just fun to see what the person is actually like. They can be anyone they want to be when you just meet them face-to-face. But on Facebook, it gives you more of a personal connection."

Chapter 5 | Tying It All Together

SYMPHONY ORCHESTRA

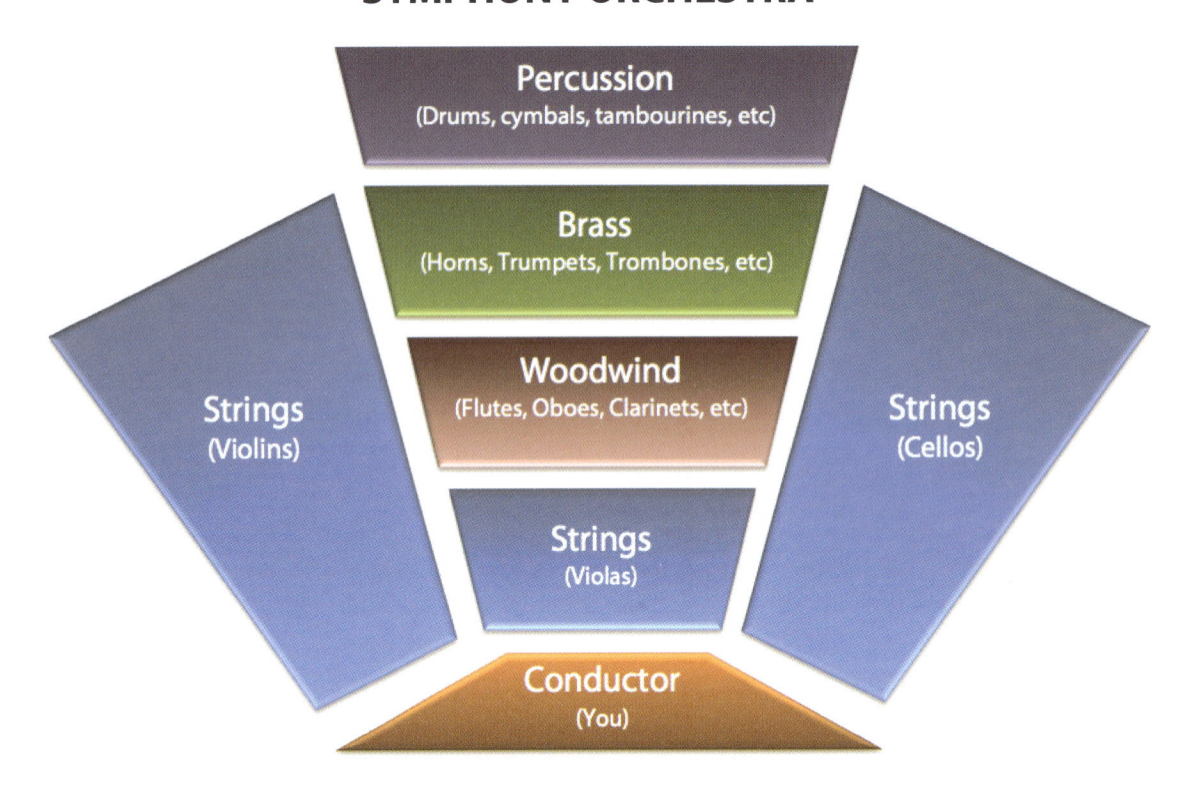

- Percussion (Drums, cymbals, tambourines, etc)
- Brass (Horns, Trumpets, Trombones, etc)
- Woodwind (Flutes, Oboes, Clarinets, etc)
- Strings (Violins)
- Strings (Cellos)
- Strings (Violas)
- Conductor (You)

SOCIAL MEDIA ORCHESTRA

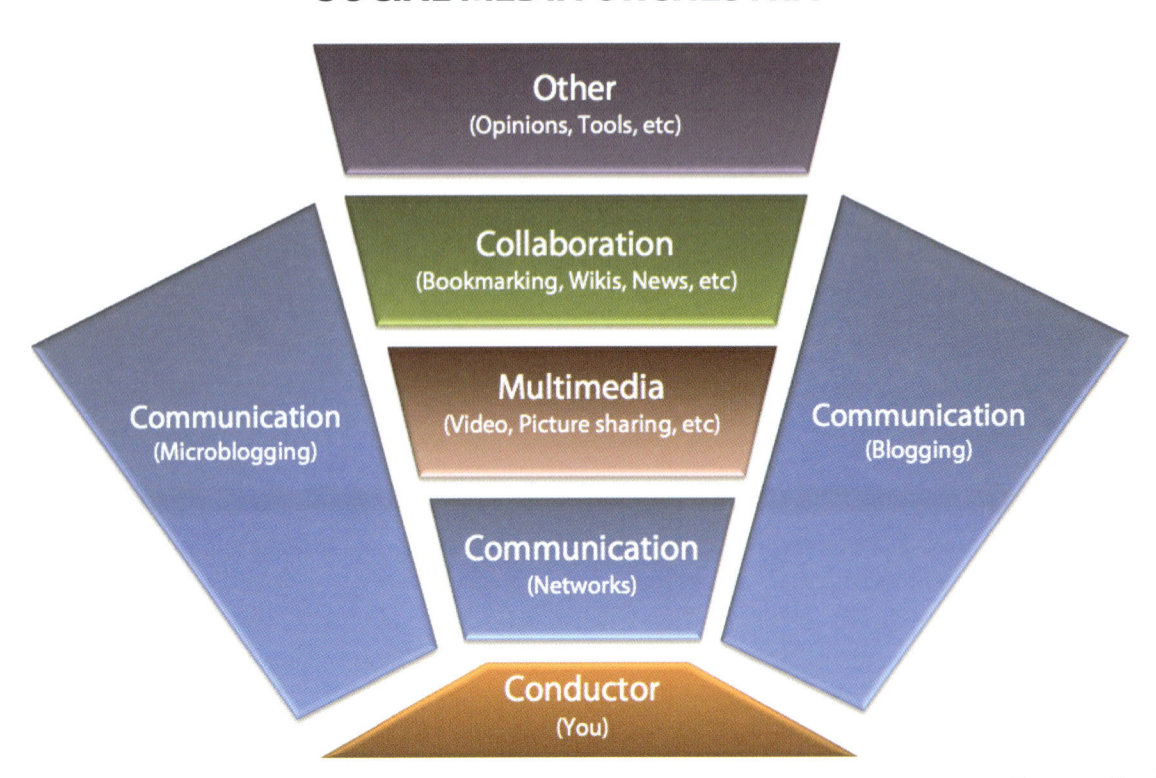

- Other (Opinions, Tools, etc)
- Collaboration (Bookmarking, Wikis, News, etc)
- Multimedia (Video, Picture sharing, etc)
- Communication (Microblogging)
- Communication (Blogging)
- Communication (Networks)
- Conductor (You)

Source: RealSure

Social Media Orchestra

To help simplify your Social Media Orchestra it has been divided into the different sections and their primary components. Then the leading service providers in each of those sections are identified.

5.2 Communication Focus

Communication is a broad term used to describe the transferring of information from one source to another. It is generally broken down into three parts: body language, voice tonality and content. However, when dealing with communication in the digital realms of Social Media it is difficult (although not impossible) to express yourself using your body language or your voice tonality. At the best of times, communication is a difficult skill to master. With Social Media it now becomes even more difficult as we are predominantly limited to content. How you share that content with others, whether you share it with one person or with many people, establishes different divisions of information distribution.

The use of sites such as Facebook and Twitter has enabled individuals to connect with others across vast distances. As such they have become deeply embedded in the user's life. This makes the Communication Focus unique and distinguishes it from the other categories as the User Category.

The three divisions of Communication Focus—Networks, Microblogging and Blogging—much like the three parts of the string section—Violas, Violins and Cellos—are the most prominent and visible when viewing the orchestra; see diagram.

Networks

As the first and most prominent tier of the Communications Focus, Networks (social or business) are very similar to the traditional offline-communities that people with common interests created: Boys & Girls Club, Kiwanis, Sierra Club, etc. Online is no different. People forming or belonging to groups and Social Networks have become the collective term to describe many of these communities such as Facebook and MySpace.

Blogging

Conversation through blogging is a large part of the Communications Focus. Although most blogs allow individuals to leave comments; a number of them do not. Either that or the posting style of the author is more of an announcement type rather than a communication type. Blog writers should write posts that entice discussion and therefore comments. Two examples of prominent multi-user blogs in the Real Estate Industry are AgentGenius (agentgenius.com) and RealBlogging (realblogging.com)

Microblogging

Microblogging is the form of communication designed around short bursts and short messages; often limited to 140 characters. It is used to provide status updates or to invite people to another location such as a website. The dominant player in this category is Twitter with Posterous (posterous.com) as the latest addition to this field.

There are hundreds of Mircoblogging sites/services. Here is a list of 10 of the most well known beyond Twitter

- Shout'Em (shoutem.com)
- Buzzable (buzzable.com)
- You Are (youare.com)
- Jaiku (jaiku.com)
- Identi.ca (identi.ca)
- Thumbcast (thumbcast.com)
- Ping.fm (ping.fm)
- Present.ly (present.ly)
- Yammer (yammer.com)
- Qaiku (qaiku.com)

5.3 Multimedia Focus

Multimedia Focus is content that uses a combination of different forms and is used in contrast to media that only uses traditional forms of printed or hand-produced material. While it includes a combination of text, audio, still images, animation and video content it also represents the convergence of all the content into a single form.

The Multimedia Focus can also be split into three divisions: Video, Photos and Music and Virtual Worlds. This is much like how the woodwind section of an orchestra contains multiple instruments—Flutes, Oboes and Clarinets. However, in both orchestras they are collected together in one location. This is especially true in Social Media as they represent a combination of various media forms.

Video

The first and most prominent tier of the Multimedia Focus is Video. Considered the most personal form of multimedia, video has allowed users to become producers by allowing them to create video diaries (commonly called vlogs). With the advent of smart phones with video camera recording and Internet capabilities, video sharing is increasing in popularity as notable video sharing sites like YouTube see a rise in mobile content.

> **There are hundreds of video sharing sites/services. Here is a list of 10 of the most well known beyond YouTube**
>
> - **MySpace Video (vids.myspace.com)**
> - **Daily Motion (dailymotion.com)**
> - **MetaCafe (metacafe.com)**
> - **TinyPic (tinpic.com)**
> - **Esnips (esnips.com)**
> - **Flurl (flurl.com)**
> - **Vimeo (vimeo.com)**
> - **Revver (revver.com)**
> - **Videojug (videojug.com)**
> - **Viddler (viddler.com)**

SUCCESS STORY

Just wanted to share a "twist" I wasn't expecting when I joined Facebook. After I added Facebook as a contact option on my Web site, I started getting friend requests from past & present clients. One of my sellers who had been having a difficult time selling her home joined my page. I was a little apprehensive, not knowing what to expect. But when they got an offer on their house - she put a huge thank you to me on her wall, telling all her friends if they need a good Realtor to call me! Once the deal was finalized, she did it a second time with incredible words of kindness. She regularly posts her progress with packing, etc. and when I join the thread her FB friends reply to my posts and now know who I am. Her use of FB turned out to be an unexpected and priceless client testimonial and created a sphere of influence (her friends and family) that now know me, and that I would not otherwise have had access to.

Sue Rossi
RE/MAX 2000, Crete IL

Photos and Music

This division of Multimedia Focus generally refers to all forms of online music and photo sharing. A popular example of an online photo-sharing site is Flickr.

Virtual Worlds

The third division of the Multimedia Focus refers to Virtual (or computer-simulated) Worlds. These worlds present perceptual stimuli to the user, who in turn can manipulate elements of the virtual world. The model world may simulate rules based on the real world or some hybrid fantasy world. Example rules are gravity, topography, locomotion, real-time actions and communication. Communication between users includes text messaging, graphical icons, visual gestures, sound and voice command. Second Life is an example of a virtual world.

> "Any effective PR or marketing strategy must in the future include social media as a core ingredient."
>
> *-Stefan Swanepoel*
> Author, Speaker & Visionary

5.4 Collaboration Focus

Collaboration Focus is a recursive process where two or more users collaborate in an intersection of common goals. An example would be an intellectual endeavor of sharing knowledge, learning and building consensus. Unlike Communication Focus, Collaboration Focus centers more on knowledge and information. Contrary to the user-focused platform where pages or profiles are established around individuals or groups, the information-focused platforms are created around terms, events, interests and/or information.

This category can also be divided into three divisions, but unlike the Communication Focus that is the most prominent and therefore divided into three sections visually, Collaboration Focus is all contained within one section. However, that does not remove the importance of its different divisions—Bookmarking, News and Events and Wikis.

Bookmarking

Bookmarking is a method for Internet users to store, organize, search and manage their webpage bookmarks. Many social bookmarking services provide web feeds and alerts for a user's lists of bookmarks. This allows subscribers to become aware of new bookmarks as they are saved, shared and tagged by other users. StumbleUpon is an example of a bookmarking service.

There are hundreds of bookmaking sites/servces. Here is a list of 10 of the most well known

- Digg (digg.com)
- Yahoo Buzz (buzz.yahoo.com)
- Stumbleupon (stumbleupon.com)
- Reddit (reddit.com)
- Technorati (technorati.ca)
- Delicious (delicious.com)
- Propeller (propeller.com)
- Simply (simply.com)
- Blogmarks (blogmarks.net)
- Newsvine (newsvine.com)

News and Events

This division focuses on news and events that are not generated via the mainstream news organizations. The value of news and events in this division are generally determined through a ranking or rating system.

Dominant players in this category are often times also bookmarking services. An example of such a combination is Digg or Delicious.

Wikis

A prominent division of the Collaboration Focus is the Wiki division. Focused around a particular interest, Wikis (from the Hawaiian word for quickly, in reference to how often updates occur) allow many individuals to participate in the production of a long-term knowledge repository or database. Two common examples of Wikis, or online encyclopedias, are Wikipedia and RealEstateWiki.

Collaboration in Social Media involves a natural, genuine conversation between people about something of mutual interest. It's about sharing and arriving at a collective point, often for the purpose of making a better or more informed choice that distinguishes the Collaboration Focus.

5.5 Other

This section of the orchestra caters to the remaining set of pieces that either do not fit in any of the aforementioned sections or are not critical in the success of your Social Media development.

5.6 Finding the Social Balance

Multimedia and the Internet require a completely new approach to writing. The writing style that is appropriate for the "on-line world" is highly optimized and designed to be quickly scanned by readers. As a result the Multimedia Focus is often distinguished as the Self-expression Category.

Again, it's not vital that you activate or participate in every section and there is no reason that you can't start one section at a time. There is no right or wrong here, neither is there a deadline or time frame. This example of a Social Media Orchestra is to illustrate that you are in control of your own participation and that it can be done piecemeal and on your own timeline.

Chapter 6

10-Day Action Plan

Introduction

The following quick start program provides suggested daily Social Media activities. If you follow them diligently, you will, after 10 days, have completed the following:

- Established your blog.
- Posted at least three blog articles.
- Begun establishing a following of readers to your blog.
- Established accounts in each of the following outposts: Twitter, Facebook, LinkedIn, YouTube.
- Added approximately 200 new "followers" (and quite possibly more) to your Twitter profile.
- Begun establishing a conversation history that will be visible to hundreds of new connections across all your social networks.

Though the following program lists 10 days of activities, it's not intended that you simply stop at the end of Day 10. "Wash, rinse, repeat" as they say and continue the activities that will have hopefully by then become daily habits.

Make no mistake; Social Media requires work and lots of time. Social connections don't "just happen" after signing up for accounts on popular Social Media platforms. Commitment, consistency and the spirit of sharing informative, helpful content are keys to your success. But, it is also true that as you settle into your daily routine, the activities will come much more smoothly. Be open to suggestions, tips and techniques you find from others online and add other activities as you become comfortable.

Above all, remember at the core of Social Media is the conversation. Meet new friends, be active in the community, offer help and specialized expertise when it is needed. This shouldn't be a new concept to you. After all, you're a real estate professional.

Good luck!

Chapter 6 | 10-Day Action Plan

☑ Day 1

General

Re-read Chapter 2 (Where to Star) and Chapter 3.1 – 3.5. ☐

Write the following:

➤ A purpose statement for your social networking activities. ☐

➤ Decide on your online persona for your social networking activities. ☐

➤ Identify your target audience, demographics, geographical market, etc. ☐

➤ Select the photo that you are going to use in all of your social networking activities. ☐

➤ Decide how much time and when you are going to spend time on your social networking activities. ☐

Your Blog

➤ Set up a blog (if you haven't already done so). Both Wordpress.com and Blogger.com offer free options. ☐

➤ Create and publish the "About" page on your blog. This page should be conversational in tone. In a few short paragraphs, this page should describe you, your services, who it is written for and how visitors can subscribe to receive your updates. You should give information about where to find your blog's RSS feed or email subscription form. ☐

Don't be anxious. We will get to all the Networks soon enough. Twitter starts tomorrow and the others below follow later:

Facebook

You Tube

LinkedIn

☑ Day 2

General

- Re-read Chapter 3.8 (Twitter) as well as Chapter 4.

- Establish your Listening Posts. This will involve signing up for accounts on each of the following:

    - RSS feeds (use Google.com/reader, for example)

    - Google.com/alerts

    - Boardreader.com

Your Blog

- Today we plan the post. Tomorrow we post.

- Think about the message you would like to share. You could start by paraphrasing your

- "About" page introducing yourself (and/or your team) and your purpose statement. Alternatively you can share with your readers what you hope to accomplish with this blog. See the end of this chapter for blog ideas. Consider a catchy title with suitable keywords that apply to your post as well as a visually striking image.

Twitter

- Set up your Twitter account. When considering an appropriate Twitter name, keep in mind that the 140 character limitation for some tweets include the length of your Twitter name.

- Make sure to complete a one-line bio for yourself and upload your photo. You have a much better chance of someone accepting your follow request if they can see who they are connecting with.

- Consider using one of the many free Twitter background applications such as Twitbacks to spruce up your Twitter page.

☑ Day 3

General

➤ Scan your RSS feed and your Listening Posts alerts. ☐

➤ Scan for conversations that mention topics of interest to you and relevant to your professional niche or geographical market. Make sure that articles/posts/conversations are relatively recent. ☐

Your Blog

➤ Post your first blog article. ☐

➤ In an effort to enhance your blog article consider adding an image that fits with your post. ☐

Twitter

➤ Post your first 2-3 tweets. Tweet links to blog articles you think may be of interest to your target audience. ☐

➤ An easy way and quick way to tweet is to retweet (RT) other people's tweets. Remember to always acknowledge the source. ☐

➤ Visit free Twitter directory applications such as Twellow. First add yourself to the Twellow directory. Then research the categories and demographics you find interesting and follow at least 20-40 people. ☐

➤ You can also follow the authors at @Swanepoel and @MelAclaro and we will gladly follow you back. ☐

Facebook starts tomorrow. The other two will follow shortly:

LinkedIn

YouTube

☑ Day 4

General

- ➤ Re-read Chapter 3.6 (Facebook). ☐

- ➤ Scan your RSS feed and Listening Posts alerts. Going forward this should be a regular part of your daily activities. ☐

- ➤ Refine your Listening Post settings based on the quantity and applicability you received. ☐

Your Blog

- ➤ Depending on how your blog and Listening Posts were set up, you may have been notified that someone commented on your blog or that a related topic was posted elsewhere. As a precaution visit your blog and check to see if you have received any comments. Set aside any relevant information you found for future blog posts. ☐

Twitter

- ➤ Post at least 5 tweets or retweets. ☐

- ➤ Follow another 20-40 people in your target audience. ☐

- ➤ View your followers tab and check for new followers. Check their profiles and unless they appear inappropriate, follow them back. ☐

- ➤ Send thank you tweets or direct messages (DM) to your new followers. ☐

Facebook

- ➤ Create a Facebook account. ☐

- ➤ Create an initial profile, include more detailed information about yourself under the "Info" tab and also upload your photo. ☐

- ➤ Post your first entry on your Facebook wall by extracting a short summary from your blog article and add a link back to the post. ☐

LinkedIn starts tomorrow. YouTube will follow after that.

✅ Day 5

General

➤ Re-read Chapter 3.8 (LinkedIn). ☐

➤ Re-Scan your RSS feed and Listening Posts alerts. ☐

Your Blog

➤ Review the topics of the end of this Chapter for ideas on your next blog. You can also consider any relevant information you set aside from Listening Posts, comments, etc. ☐

➤ Write and post your next blog article. ☐

Twitter

➤ Repeat the Twitter activities of yesterday. ☐

➤ Remember to also check your DMs daily and respond to messages. ☐

➤ Visit 3-5 profiles of interesting people that you would like to build a relationship with and comment on one of their tweets. ☐

Facebook

➤ Import your Personal Email Address Book and see which of your existing contacts are already on Facebook. Send Facebook friend invites to them. ☐

➤ Update your Facebook status by answering the question, "What's on your mind?" in the space provided at the top of your profile. These can include links to blog posts, articles or videos. (Be creative in a professionally-appropriate manner). ☐

LinkedIn

➤ Go to LinkedIn and open a free account. LinkedIn will become your online resume page so make sure it is professional. ☐

➤ Complete your entire LinkedIn profile until the profile shows 100% complete. ☐

➤ Browse the Company Directory by Category and search for people that you know. Find at least 10-20 to start with and send them an invitation to connect with you. Your are welcome to connect with both of the authors on LinkedIn by merely searching for our names. ☐

☑ Day 6

General

- Reread Chapter 3.9 (YouTube). ☐
- Scan your RSS feed and Listening Posts alerts. ☐

Your Blog

- Think about your next blog post. ☐

Twitter

- Repeat your Twitter daily activities. ☐

Facebook

- Add a photo album with 5-10 photos that are aligned with your motivation and purpose. ☐
- Tag (name) the people in the photos and write captions for each photo. ☐
- Check to see if you have received any friend requests, accept the appropriate ones. ☐
- Visit their profiles and then post on their wall a message indicating your enthusiasm to connect via Facebook. ☐
- Search their friends list and see if there are any other people you know. Try and add a minimum of 20 potential new friends per day. For example you can befriend co-author Mel Aclaro. ☐

LinkedIn

- Update your LinkedIn status where it says "What are you working on?" ☐
- Remember to add in all your websites, blogs, Twitter profile, Facebook page and YouTube page. ☐

YouTube

- Go to YouTube, sign up for a free account. ☐
- Fill out the information about who you are. Design the layout of your channel to match your purpose statement. ☐
- To grow your YouTube channel start subscribing to other channels (same as following someone on Twitter). Find 5-10 channels that you believe are valuable and relevant. ☐

✓ Day 7

General

➤ Scan your RSS feed and Listening Posts alerts. ☐

Your Blog

➤ Follow as standard routine of reviewing comments on your posts, setting aside good information from your Listening Posts and thinking about your next blog article. ☐

Twitter

➤ Repeat your Twitter daily activities. ☐

Facebook

➤ Search groups and fan pages that may be relevant to your business, service, market, etc. Remember to check for company names, cities names, your franchise, your Realtor® Assn. etc. ☐

➤ You can use the Search function, or see what Groups and Fan pages your friends belong to. You are invited to join the fan page of co-author Stefan Swanepoel at www.Facebook.com/swanepoelinternational ☐

➤ Continue adding 10-20 or so friends per day, writing on their walls and commenting on their posts. ☐

LinkedIn

➤ Find at least 10-20 people and send them an invitation to connect with you. Browse the Groups Directory by Category such as Alumni, Non-Profit, Corporate, etc and search for former or current groups you may belong to. Continue your search for people you know by looking at the connections of your contacts to see who they are connected to. ☐

YouTube

➤ If you have any videos already available go ahead and add them. Be aware of copyright and plagiarism. ☐

➤ Scan YouTube for videos that are interesting and "favorite" them. Add comments where applicable. ☐

➤ Look for possible good ideas to make your own video. ☐

☑ Day 8

General

➤ Scan your RSS feed and Listening Posts alerts. ☐

Your Blog

➤ Post your next blog article. ☐

Twitter

➤ You should now typically every day be posting 3-5 tweets, retweeting 3-5 times, adding 40+ followers, sending or responding to 10-20 DMs, etc. ☐

Facebook

➤ Update your Facebook status. ☐

➤ Continue adding 10-20 friends per day, writing on their walls and commenting on their posts. Add the free Facebook application "NetworkedBlogs". Go to http://apps.facebook.com/blognetworks/ and follow the instructions. ☐

LinkedIn

➤ Check your inbox for acceptances by Groups you joined previously and start participating by posting comments on those pages. ☐

YouTube

➤ YouTube is all about broadcasting yourself, your company, service, etc. Begin mapping it out the message you wish to convey. Remember to also consider things such as background, props, length of video, closing words, website address to be provided, etc. ☐

➤ At the same time, to make your future video will be popular, consider what conversation you wish to create around the video, any questions to be posted, comments, etc. ☐

Chapter 6 | 10-Day Action Plan

☑ Day 9

General

- ➤ Re-read Chapter 5 (Tying it all Together and "Become the Conductor"). ☐

- ➤ Scan your RSS feed and Listening Posts alerts. ☐

Your Blog

- ➤ Consider inviting another person to provide you a guest article for your blog. ☐

Twitter

- ➤ Repeat your Twitter regular activities. ☐

- ➤ Start adding other activities such as participating in hashtags (for example #FollowFriday). ☐

Facebook

- ➤ Post regular entries on your wall, comment on the walls of friends, send out more friend requests, respond to people who accepted your friend request, visit groups and fan pages aligned with your purpose statement, check your inbox for emails, etc. ☐

- ➤ Try and always add value to your friends. Create conversation by asking questions and sharing your opinions. ☐

LinkedIn

- ➤ Start investigating some of the many other LinkedIn tools such as LinkedIn Answers. ☐

YouTube

- ➤ Use a video camera, webcam or flip cam to record your first video. If appropriate edit. ☐

- ➤ Make sure you come up with an appropriate title, relevant keywords and a good description. Add links in the description to articles, pictures or videos you may reference in your video. ☐

- ➤ Post to YouTube. You can also use one of the paid services such as TrafficGeyser to submit your video to tens of other video sites simultaneously. ☐

☑ Day 10

General

➤ By now you should feel comfortable with the purpose of your Social Media activities and starting to find your voice. Continue to publish, blog, post or tweet with regularity. Most experts recommend 60-90 minutes per day if you wish to grow and maintain a strong and effective Social Media presence. ☐

Your Blog

➤ Invite customers, partners, vendors, etc. to read, share and contribute to your blog. ☐

➤ Constantly be on the look out for other successful blogs to what you can do, add, change, etc. to improve your blog. Research blog tools and apps that could enhance you blog. ☐

➤ Remember that you can also add video to future blog articles. ☐

Twitter

➤ Repeat your Twitter regular activities. ☐

➤ Investigate desktop applications such as Hootsuite and Tweetdeck that enables you to manage Twitter more effectively. ☐

Facebook

➤ Posting entries on your wall, commenting on other peoples' walls, inviting friends, acknowledging new friends, etc. should now be a normal daily activity for you. ☐

LinkedIn

➤ LinkedIn does not require daily maintenance as the other Social Media networks but keep your information current at all times. ☐

YouTube

➤ For future videos continue to explore ideas and events, talk about something relevant to your purpose statement, inform viewers about your experience and opinion, etc. ☐

➤ Remember to post your YouTube video link in your blog, on Facebook, Twitter, etc. If people don't know your video is there many may never see it. ☐

Blog Suggestions

To help spark your creative juices consider some of the following as possible blog articles:

- *Champion another blogger.* In this type of article, it will help you to scan articles posted by other bloggers. Find an article that resonates with you and write your thoughts about it in 2 or 3 paragraphs. Include a link to the other blog article in the body of your post.

- *Champion a client.* In this type of article—and with permission from your client—write a blog article about the unique challenges in a recent real estate transaction. Relate these challenges to those your prospects (visitors to your blog site) would be wise to consider. Consider also describing how your expertise and understanding of the local market were instrumental in the successful resolution of your client's challenges.

- *Write a Review-type post.* This can be a few paragraphs reviewing a book you have recently read, a community in your farm, local business, restaurant or service provider in your area. This type of article is a great opportunity to "spread the wealth" by giving visibility to a local service provider (e.g., home inspector, carpet cleaner, painter, handyman, etc.) who may have provided exceptional service during one of your recent transactions.

- *Write a How To type post.* This can be a few paragraphs explaining a topic in which you are knowledgeable. For example, the real estate purchase/listing process, explanations of purchase contract contingencies, highlights of a 1031 exchange, short sales in a nutshell, etc.

- *Write an opinion post.* This will be a topic about which you have some expertise. Example: Opinion about how housing inventory will impact home prices in your area, or a summary of discussions from your recent branch/office meeting, etc.

- *Write an answer post.* In this type of post, you will answer a question. These can be from a list of "frequently asked questions" buyers, sellers and prospects typically ask. Another variation to consider is to scan/search for questions in LinkedIn Answers. Use your blog to answer the question found in LinkedIn. Then, paraphrase your blog answer in the appropriate LinkedIn area where the question was asked. Consider also including a link back to your blog post to invite others on LinkedIn to read your detailed response.

- *Write a "top x" post.* In this type of post, you will write an article that list the "top x" of some topic. For example, "The top 5 reasons homes stay on the market longer." Or, "The top 4 reasons buyers overpay for real estate."

- *Write a video-embedded post.* In this type of post, you will write a blog article that includes an embedded video from one of those you have previously "favorited" to your YouTube profile page. With the video, include a paragraph or two describing why you are sharing it. (E.g., For fun? Because it relates to a frequently asked client topic? Etc.)

As you can see from the bullet points above, there are many more ways to add value without turning your blog into yet another marketing slick for your listings. By changing the mix and providing informative, insightful and helpful posts such as those above, you will find yourself quickly differentiating yourself from other real estate agents who may not have been privy to these tips.

Conclusion

As suggested at the beginning of Chapter 6, once you have successfully complete the first 10 days of this quick start program, you must continue on with your daily routine. You should by now start to see the benefits of integrating the different parts of the Social Media Orchestra.

Although you are only coordinating five Social Media services in your Orchestra today, we are sure that you are probably already overwhelmed and pressed for time. We understand, so we will not be adding more, this year. For now, just stay the course. With diligence and commitment you will soon find your own rhythm and will be well on your way to online socializing with more purpose, focus and ultimately a return on your investment (time).

As the *Swanepoel SOCIAL MEDIA Report* is an annual publication we look forward to sharing with you next year another five Social Media platforms you should consider adding to your Orchestra. We will also be discussing the most up-to-date innovations and which applications we recommend you use to maximize your Social Media Orchestra even better.

To friends, followers and fans …we look forward to connecting with you online in the new world of Social Media.

References

References

Books, Magazines, Online News, Presentations and Studies

ActiveRain. (2009). Retrieved from ActiveRain.com

AgentGenius (2009) Retrieved from AgentGenius

Arrington, M. (2009). *Twitter Mania: Google Got Shut Down. Apple Rumors Heat Up.* Retrieved from TechCrunch.com

Bachraty, R. (2009). *Social Media Karma.* Retrieved from Truliablog

BBC News. (2009). *Twitter hype punctured by study.*

Berman, A. (2009). *Iran's Twitter Revolution.* Retrieved from The Nation

Boyd, D. M., & Ellison, N. (2007). Social Network Sites: Definition, History and Scholarship. *Journal of Computer-Mediated Communication*, 13 (1).

Boyd, D. M. (2009). Social Media is Here to Stay... Now What? *Microsoft Research Tech Fest.* Redmond, Washington, United State of America.

Branther, E. (2008). *The 11 Rules of Social Media Etiquette.* Retrieved from Digital Labz

Busari, S. (2008). *Tweeting the terror: How social media reacted to Mumbai.* Retrieved from CNN

Chaney, P. (2009). *The Digital Handshake: Seven Proven Strategies to Grow Your Business Using Social Media*

Chimire, S. (2008). *Social Media Quote of the Day.* Retrieved 2009 from Social Media Biz

CNN Money. (2007). *Business 2.0 - How to Succeed in 2007.*

Comm, J. (2009). *Twitter Power: How to Dominate Your Market One Tweet at a Time.* Wiley.

comScore. (2009). *YouTube Surpasses 100 Million US Viewers for the First Time.* Retrieved from comScore

Covey, S. (1990). *The 7 Habits of Highly Effective People.* Free Press.

Crain Communications. (2009). *Digital Marketing and Media Fact Pack.*

Drumgoole, J. (2006). *Web 2.0 vs Web 1.0.* Retrieved from Copacetic

Eaton, F. (2009). Web 2.0 and You. Retrieved from Examiner.com

Edmond, D. (2008). *Six Key Elements of an Effective Social Media Strategy.* Retrieved from KoMarketing Associates

Evans, D. (2008). *Social Media Marketing.* Wiley Publishing, Inc.

Fisch, K. (2008). *Did You Know 3.0.* Retrieved from YouTube

flickr. (2008). *3 Billion!* Retrieved from Flickr

Gobie, G. (2009). *The History of Social Networking.* Retrieved from Digital Trends

Hahn, R. (2009). *3 Social Media Myths.* Retrieved from Inman News.

Hitwise. (2009). *Top 20 Social Networking Websites.* Retrieved from Hitwise

Inman News (2009). Retrieved from Inman News

Jay. (2009). *Facebook Social Ads: The New Adwords*

Kitano, P. (2009). *Social Media Feeds SEO.* Retrieved from TransparentRE

Lange, P. G. (2007). P*ublicly Private and Privately Public: Social Networking on YouTube*

LinkedIn. (2009). *About Us.* Retrieved from LinkedIn

LiveJournal. (2009). *Our Company.* Retrieved from LIveJournal

MadV. (2007). *The Message.* From YouTube

MarketingSavant. (2009). *Marketech Tools and Trends in Marketing Technology*

Meisel, L. (2008). *YouTube's Political Revolution.* Retrieved from Breakthrough Institute

Miniwatts Marketing Group. (2009). *Internet Growth Statistics.* Retrieved from Internet World Stats

Morozov, E. (2009). *Moldova's Twitter Revolution.* Retrieved from Foreign Policy

NewsGeni.us (2009) Retrieved from NewsGeni.us

Nicolay, Nicole. (2009) *Twitter for Real Estate Twits.* Retrieved from MyTechOpinion.com

O'Malley, G. (2009). *Superconnected: 71 Percent Say They Can't Live Without Facebook.* Retrieved from Media Post

O'Neil, N. (2009). *Exploring the Long Tail of Facebook Pages.* Retrieved from AllFacebook.com

Phillips, S. (2007). *A brief history of Facebook.* Retrieved from The Guardian

Qualman, E. (2009). *Social Media Revolution.* Retrieved from YouTube

RandomHistory. (2008). *"A Place for Friends" - A History of MySpace.* Retrieved from RandomHistory.com

RealEstateWiki. (2009). Retrieved from RealEstatewiki.com

RealEstateZebra. (2009). Retrieved from RealEstateZebra.com

Realtors.org. (2009). Retrieved from Realtors.org

Rivlin, G. (2006). *Wallflower at the Web Party.* Retrieved from The New York Times

Ross, J.M. (2009). *A Corporate Guide for Social Media.* Retrieved from Forbes.com

Rothamel, D. (2007). *Welcome to Social Media for Real Estate 101: Twitter.* Retrieved from ActiveRain

Singer, A. (2009). *10 Reasons Why Social Is Your Future SEO Strategy.* Retrieved from The Future Buzz

Sherman, A. (2009). *10 Golden Rules of Social Media.* Retrieved from Web Worker Daily

Shumaker, D. (2009). *Will You Be My Friend???* Information Central Presented at NAR.

Solis, B., & Thomas, J. (2008). The Conversation Prism. Retrieved from The Conversation Prism

References

Stiles, A. (2009, March 18). *Graphing Total Daily Tweets.* Retrieved from AdamStiles.com

Swanepoel, S. *Swanepoel Trends Report 2008 & 2009.* RealSure.

Wesch, M. (2009). *Anthropology of YouTube.* Retrieved July 6, 2009 from YouTube Biz Blog

Wikipedia. (2009). From Wikipedia.org

Williams, A. (2009). *Podcasting Made Easy.*

Ziberg, C. (2009). *On July 30, Plaxo begins charging the now free Outlook syncing $60 a year – will you pay?* Retrieved from Geek.com

Zuckerberg, M. (2009, April 8). *200 Million Strong.* Retrieved from Facebook

Zuckerberg, M. (2009, July 15). *Now Connecting 250 Million People.* Retrieved from Facebook

Glossary

Social Media Glossary

Adsense - Google's pay-per-click, context-relevant program available as a way to create revenue.

Adwords - The advertiser program that populates the Adsense program. The advertiser pays Google on a per click basis.

Aggregators - Web sites that bring together content and links from many different sites around the internet.

Aggregation - Gathering and remixing of content from various sources such as blogs, RSS feeds, etc. Good examples include Bloglines or Google Reader.

Akismet - Comment spam filter popular with WordPress blogs.

Alerts - The ability to have external search engines search for specific words, phrases or tags that you want to monitor. Those results are then sent to you via email. A good example would be Google Alerts.

Atom - A popular feed format used for syndicating content.

Authenticity -The sense that something or someone is "real." When publishing content and engaging in conversations, try and show that your interest and values are sincere and real.

Avatar - A 2D- or 3D customized graphical image used in virtual world to represent people.

Back Channel Communications - Private emails or other messages sent by the facilitator or between individuals during conferencing.

Blogosphere - Complete collection of all blogs on the Internet and the conversations that take place within that sphere.

Blogs - Shortened from the original term "Weblog." It is an article or entry that is dated and usually extends beyond 400 characters or a paragraph in length. A good example of a blog is Blogger or Wordpress.

Blogroll - List of sites displayed in the sidebar of a blog showing who the blogger reads regularly.

Bookmarking - Saving the address of a Website or piece of content in either your browser or on a social bookmarking site such as Delicious.

Browser - Tool used to access online content and websites. Some examples of browsers include Firefox, Internet Explorer, Chrome and Safari.

Bulletin Boards - Early platform for online collaboration where users connected with a central computer to post and read email-like messages or articles.

Chat - Real time interaction on a website with multiple individuals adding comments via text entries.

Collaborate - Means the cooperation of different people to use the combined knowledge or wisdom of the group; often done in wikis.

Comments - Feedback added under blog posts and other content.

Community Building - The process of recruiting potential community or network participants, helping them to find shared interests and goals and using technology to develop useful conversations.

CGM - Consumer-generated media refers to the first content created including blogs, video-sharing, etc. that is then posted or shared across a variety of platforms.

CMS - A Content Management System that is used to input web or blog content.

Conversation - The act of commenting or contributing to forums and discussions via a social networking or Social Media platform.

Copyright - Sharing through Social Media is enhanced by attaching a Creative Commons license specifying, for example, that content may be re-used with attribution, provided that a similar license is then attached by the new author.

Crowdsourcing -Posing a question to a large group of people online to try to get to the best answer quickly.

Dashboard - The administration area on your blog software that allows you to post, check traffic, upload files, manage comments, etc.

DM - Direct Messages are private messages sent from one individual to another on Twitter.

Embed - A way of linking to content (often video) so that the content itself is visible on (embedded into) the page itself.

Entry - An individual post published on a blog. Each of these entries, while appearing in an index, are also web pages themselves.

Feed - A string of content sent by an aggregator that you can read, view or listen to; coming from blogs, podcasts and other RSS-enabled sites without visiting the site. A good example would be Bloglines.

FeedBurner - A tool allowing web sites, blogs and podcasts to "burn" content into a simple way for readers to subscribe.

Feed Reader - An aggregator of content, subscribed to by the user, so that specific content or search results arrives in their "reader".

Hashtag - Similar to regular tags, these are keywords associated and assigned to an item of content with a hash mark (#) attached to the front of the word. Mainly used in Twitter.

Glossary

HTML - Acronym for HyperText Markup Language, the coding language used to create and link together documents and files on the World Wide Web. The code is embedded in and around text and multimedia files in order to define layout, font, colors, and graphics.

Hub - The center of your Internet and Social Media strategy to which you drive or send traffic, people, customers, etc. with which you wish to expand your relationship. Good examples would be your website or your blog.

Hyperlink - A navigational reference to another document or page on the World Wide Web.

Listening Posts - Places or stations that you subscribe to or partake in that search, find, categorize and return to you information on topics, people, companies, etc., about which you whish to remain knowledgeable. Good example would be Google Alerts.

Long Tail - Reference to the high value of smaller groups of individuals with significant interest in a service or product as compared to the low value of larger groups with little interest in the service or product.

Mashup - A web application that combines data from more than one source into a single tool.

Message Boards - A web application for holding discussions and posting user generated content to an entire community usually dealing with a distinct topic.

Microblogging - Short blogging entries/posts that are usually limited to 140-200 characters. Twitter is a good example of a microblog.

Moblog - A blog published directly to the web from a mobile device.

Mobile Marketing - Description of marketing on, with or to a mobile device such as a phone or PDA.

Online Community - A group of people that interact via the web rather traditional communication media such as letters, telephone or face to face.

Open-source software - Refers to any software whose source code is available under a license that permits users to study, change, improve and then redistribute the software.

Outposts - Creating places on the Internet and in Social Media networks whereby you have a method to communicate with people, your customer or following.

Photosharing - Sharing of your images through a website. You can add tags and offer people the opportunity to comment or even reuse your photos.

Ping - "Packet Internet Group" or "Packed Internet Gopher." This refers to an automatic notification sent when a blog has been updated. It also refers to the automatic communication between networked computers/servers.

Podcast - A digital broadcast through the Internet. The majority of podcasts are audio files sent to directories through XML feeds and RSS.

Podcasting - The term is a combination of "broadcast and "pod" referring to the distribution of a digital media file over the internet for playback on portable media players, PC or iPod.

RSS - "Really Simple Syndication" is the XML format that allows you to subscribe to content on blogs, podcasts and other Social Media and have it delivered to you through a feed.

SEO - Search engine optimization is the process of improving the volume and quality of traffic to a website from search engines via "natural" (organic or algorithmic) search results.

SMO - Acronym for Social Media Optimization.

SMS - Short messaging system; also often referred to as texting.

Social Bookmarking - The collaborative equivalent of storing favorites within a web browser and sharing those favorites with other individuals. Good examples of social bookmarking sites are Furl and Delicious.

Social Media - The term used to describe the tools and platforms people use to publish, converse and share content online. These include blogs, wikis, podcasts, networks and the sites dedicated to sharing information, stories, photos, audio and video files and bookmarks.

Social Networking - Sites developed to help people discover new friends or colleagues with shared interests, related skills or a common geographic location. It is also used to reaffirm pre-existing relationships and connections. A good example of a social networking site is Facebook.

Spambot - An automatic software robots that post spam on a blog.

Tagging - A way of categorizing online content using keywords that describe what can be found at a website, bookmark, photo or blog post.

Texting - Title given to the exchange of brief written messages between mobile phones.

Videosharing - Sharing of videos or video diaries through a website. You can discuss topics and offer people the opportunity to comment or video respond.

Vlogs - Shortened from the combined terms" video blogging." It is a diary style video entry with the user as the main focus.

Widget - A portable snippet of code that can be embedded in an HTML based web page by an end user within another blog or web site.

Twitter Glossary

Co-Twitterer - A partner that tweets on your Twitter account.

Dweet - A Tweet sent while intoxicated.

Mistweet - A tweet that one regrets later.

Neweeter - A new Tweeter.

Twadd - To add someone as a friend to Twitter.

Twaggle - A gaggle of followers.

Twaigslist - To sell something via Twitter.

Twaiting - Twittering while waiting.

Twaffic - Twitter traffic.

Twaunt - To taunt someone over Twitter.

Twead - To read a Twitter.

Twebay - To offer something for sale via Twitter.

Tweekend - Spending your entire weekend on Twitter.

Tweeple - Twitter people, Twitter members, Twitter users.

Tweepish - Feeling sheepish or regretful about something you tweeted.

Tweeps - Twitterites that follow each other from one online network to another.

Twease - A person who teases people over Twitter.

Twends - Trends caused by Twitter and micro-blogging.

Tweet-back - Bringing a previous tweet conversation back into the current conversation.

Tweet-dropping - Eavesdropping on someone's else's Home Page in With Friends mode.

Tweetaholism - The addiction to continued use of Twitter.

Tweeter - A Twitter user.

Tweeterboxes - Twitterers who tweet too much.

Tweetheart - That special someone who makes your heart skip a beat.

Twitterholic - Someone who is addicted to Twitter.

TweetIn - When a group of Twitterers agree to get together at a set time to Twitter.

Tweeting - The act of posting to Twitter.

Tweets - Posts on Twitter by Twitterers.

Tweetsult - An insult via Twitter.

TweetUp - When Twitterers meet in person in one's home nest.

Twemendous - Something fabulous that happened as a result of Twitter.

Twetiquette - The correct manner to use Twitter.

Twhepherd - The Twitter employee that finds and restores lost followers to your twaggle.

Twexplanation - Sending a nebulous Tweet and having to explain it while offline from Twitter.

Twittercal mass - A community that has achieved a critical mass of Twitterers.

Twibute - To pay tribute on Twitter.

Twis - To dis a fellow Twitterer.

Twit - Someone who doesn't follow Twitter Twettiquette.

Twisticuffs - Fighting with a fellow Twitterer over twitter.

Twitosphere - Community of Twitterers

Twittastic - Something fantastic and wonderful.

Twittcrastination - Twittering as a form of procrastination.

Twitterati - The glamorous A-List Twitterer's everyone wants to follow.

Twitterbation - When you tweet yourself.

Twitterer - A user of Twitter.

Twittectomy - Unfollowing friends.

Twittering - To send a Twitter message.

Twitterish - Erractic behavior with short outbursts.

Twittonary – Dictionary of Twitter Terms.

Twired - Tired after excessive Twittering.

Twitterfly - Being a social butterfly on Twitter.

Twitterject - Interject your tweet into an existing tweet stream of conversation.

Twitterlicious - Something delightful on Twitter.

Twitterlooing - Twittering from a bathroom.

Twitterloop - To be caught up with friend tweets and up on the conversation.

Twittermaps - A mashup technology that lets Twitter users find each other using Google maps.

Twitterpated - To be overwhelmed with Twitter messages.

Twitterphoria - The elation you feel when the person you've added as a friend adds you back.

Twitterrhea - The act of sending too many Twitter messages.

Twitterrific - A really good Tweat

Glossary

Twittervision - locates the Twitterer on a map.

Twittsomnia - Inability to sleep due to excessive Twittering.

Twittertories - Clusters of Twittererers that follow and friend each other with little overlap with other clusters.

Twittertude - Bad Twitter attitude.

Twittfessional - A confession made on Twitter.

Twitticisms - Witty Tweets.

Twittilate - To arouse with Tweets.

Twittish - Too skittish to Twitter.

Twittsomnia - Twittering due to inability to sleep.

Twittworking - Networking with Twitterites using Twitter.

Twixt - Can't decide who to Tweet.

Twhiner - A Twitterer who only ever posts whiney, negative Tweets.

Twofor - Replying to two unrelated Tweets with a single Tweet.

TwoingTwoing - To Twitter about wonderful things.

Twlocked - To have Twitter (writers) block.

Twoops - When you accidentally send a private SMS to Twitter

Twoosh - A full 140 character Twitter.

Twopsies - When you drop things because you are Twittering.

Twurvey - A survey sent out over Twitter.

Twype - To type a Twitter.

About the Authors

About Mel

Mel Aclaro is the founder of MindBridj.com; a social media company that transforms live workshops and training seminars to online learning events through the power of web video and social digital content.

In previous roles, Mel has overseen national initiatives to deliver just-in-time learning opportunities for real estate professionals in the U.S. and has been involved in education programs such as The Certified Short Sale Professional (CSP), The Certified Negotiation Expert (CNE) and Accredited Home-staging Specialist (AHS).

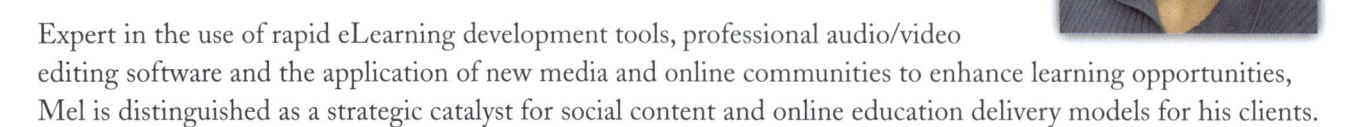

Expert in the use of rapid eLearning development tools, professional audio/video editing software and the application of new media and online communities to enhance learning opportunities, Mel is distinguished as a strategic catalyst for social content and online education delivery models for his clients.

Mel can be reached via email at Mel@MindBridj.com or online at:

Facebook — www.facebook.com/melaclaro
LinkedIn — www.linkedin.com/in/melaclaro
Twitter — www.twitter.com/melaclaro

About Stefan

Stefan Swanepoel is widely recognized as one the leading visionaries on real estate business trends, change and social media.

He has penned 15 books and reports including the best-seller Real Estate confronts Reality, the highly acclaimed annual Swanepoel TRENDS Report and the new Swanepoel SOCIAL MEDIA Report.

Stefan has received numerous recognitions such as:

- Businessman of the Year (Jaycees)
- One of the Top 25 Technology Trainers in the US (Real Estate CyberSpace Society)
- One of the Top 100 Most Influential Real Estate Leaders in 2008 (Inman News)
- One of the Top 25 Most Connected Real Estate Professionals Online in 2009 (Proxio)
- One of the Top 50 People Who You Should Follow on Twitter in 2009 (Roost)

His academic accomplishments include a bachelor's in science, a master's in business economics and diplomas in arbitration, mergers and acquisitions, real estate, computer science and marketing.

He can be reached via email at Stefan@Swanepoel.com or online at:

Facebook	–	www.facebook.com/swanepoelinternational
LinkedIn	–	www.linkedin.com/in/swanepoel
Twitter	–	www.twitter.com/swanepoel

Swanepoel
Social Media Report 2010
A Field Guide For Real Estate Professionals

Copies Item	Cover Price	Shipping Per Unit	Total Per Unit	Quantity Order	Total Price
1	$79.95	$6.95	$86.90		
2-10	$68.05	$5.95	$74.00		
11-25	$62.05	$4.95	$67.00		
26-50	$52.05	$3.95	$56.00		
50+	$43.05	$2.95	$46.00		

*Sales Tax Will be Added for California Orders

Total: _____

TO ORDER

Phone: (949) 698-2362
Online: www.RealEstateBooks.org
Mail: PO BOX 7259
Laguna Niguel
CA 92607

Name (please print clearly)

Address

City State Zip

Email Telephone

Credit Card: ☐ AmEx ☐ Visa ☐ Mastercard ☐ Discover

Credit Card Number Security Code

Signature Expiration Date

Order before Feb. 1, 2010

Pre-Pub. Price $99

Top 10 Trends
The Transition Year
FROM BABY BOOMERS TO GEN Y

*Provisional Cover

Copies Item	Unit Price	Shipping Per Unit	Total Per Unit	Quantity Order	Total Price
1	$149.95	$6.95	$156.90		
2-5	$129.95	$5.95	$135.90		
6-10	$109.95	$4.95	$114.90		
11-25	$99.95	$3.95	$103.90		
26-50	$79.95	$2.95	$82.90		
50+	$59.95	$2.95	$62.90		

*Sales Tax Will be Added for California Orders

Total: _____

TO ORDER

Phone: (949) 698-2362
Online: www.RealEstateBooks.org
Mail: PO BOX 7259
Laguna Niguel
CA 92607

Name (please print clearly)

Address

City State Zip

Email Telephone

Credit Card: ☐ AmEx ☐ Visa ☐ Mastercard ☐ Discover

Credit Card Number Security Code

Signature Expiration Date